THE NEW

Illustrated

BIBLE

THE NEW
Illustrated
BIBLE

THE GREAT STORIES OF THE BIBLE
RETOLD IN A FRESH AND LIVELY WAY
FOR TODAY

Illustrated by Diana Shimon

John Hunt
Publishing Limited

Copyright © 2003 John Hunt Publishing Ltd.

Text © 2003 Mark Water

Illustrations © 2003 Diana Shimon

ISBN 1-84298-091-2

Designed by
ANDREW MILNE DESIGN

Write to John Hunt Publishing Ltd
46a West Street, Alresford, Hampshire SO24 9AU, UK

The rights of Mark Water as author and Diana Shimon illustrator
of this work have been asserted in accordance with the Copyright,
Designs and Patents Act 1988.

A CIP catalogue record for this book is available from the British Library.

Printed in Malaysia

INTRODUCTION

The aim of The New Illustrated Bible *is to bring the Bible to life for young readers. Though it covers all the usual Bible stories, with their drama and passion, it does much more than this. The balance of text approximates to the text of the Bible itself. So weight is given to the laws of Leviticus, the Song of Solomon, and many passages usually ignored. Wisdom literature, prophecy, vision and parable are given as much space as historical adventure. In terms of story and event Balaam and Balaak are covered as well as Joshua and Caleb, Jael and Barak as well as Gideon.*

Divided into 19 chapters, each has an introduction that reveals the developing thread of the story, linking history to interpretation, literature to life. This approach roots the stories in the historical reality of their times.

The artwork is extensively researched, and indeed many of the pictures have been drawn by the Israeli artist in situ. Diana Shimon captures the bleakness of the desert, the beauty of the fields and olive groves, the tumble of village life, the work of the potters and smiths, the harsh Middle Eastern light. Side panels provide background information on artefacts and customs, writings and beliefs. Direct quotes from the Bible texts are illustrated and draw the reader into the world of the storytellers and their listeners. Bible references on each page relate the story to the main Bible text.

This is the most complete colour children's Bible available, capturing the full story of the chosen people's 1,000 year plus experience of God, and ending with its spread to the rest of the world.

CONTENTS

OLD TESTAMENT

Contents	Bible Characters	Period	Bible books	Page
CHAPTER 1 *Noah and the Great Flood*				
From the Bible book of Genesis				**17**
In the beginning	Adam and Eve		Genesis	18
The day the world changed	Cain and Abel		Genesis	20
Rain into rainbow	Noah		Genesis	23
The tower of Babel		*Unknown*	Genesis	26
Into the unknown	Abraham and Sarah		Genesis	28
A city in flames	Lot		Genesis	30
Ishmael is looked after	Hagar and Ishmael		Genesis	32
CHAPTER 2 *Abraham's amazing faith*				
From the Bible book of Genesis				**33**
God's test for Abraham	Isaac		Genesis	34
A marriage made in heaven	Rebecca		Genesis	36
A successful mission	Laban		Genesis	38
Nonidentical twins	Esau and Jacob	*2000–1900 BCE*	Genesis	40
More than a family squabble	Rebecca and Isaac		Genesis	42
Jacob leaves home	Jacob		Genesis	44
The cheat is cheated	Laban		Genesis	46
Rachel's theft	Rachel		Genesis	48

Contents	Bible Characters	Period	Bible books	Page

CHAPTER 3 *Joseph's startling dreams*
From the Bible book of Genesis — **49**

	Bible Characters	Period	Bible books	Page
Joseph the dreamer	Joseph		Genesis	50
Dreams don't seem to come true	Reuben		Genesis	52
Sold into slavery	Potiphar		Genesis	55
Joseph in prison	Waiter and baker	1700-1200 BCE	Genesis	56
A prisoner advises a king	King of Egypt		Genesis	58
Joseph's brothers come to Egypt	Joseph's 10 brothers		Genesis	60
Joseph and his brothers	Benjamin		Genesis	62
Jacob goes to Egypt	Israel (that is Jacob)		Genesis	64

CHAPTER 4 *Moses and the great escape*
From the Bible book of Exodus — **65**

	Bible Characters	Period	Bible books	Page
The Israelites grow	Moses		Exodus	66
Moses runs away from Egypt	Zipporah		Exodus	68
"Let my people go"	Aaron		Exodus	70
Miserable Moses	Moses	1250-1200 BCE	Exodus	72
Plagues galore!	King of Egypt		Exodus	74
The last plague	King of Egypt		Exodus	76
A midnight to remember	King of Egypt		Exodus	77
The great escape	Moses		Exodus	78
Songs of praise	Miriam		Exodus	80

Contents	Bible Characters	Period	Bible books	Page
CHAPTER 5 *God's people journey through the desert* From the Bible books of Exodus, Numbers, Deuteronomy and Joshua				**81**
Problems in the desert	Moses		Exodus	82
A golden calf	Aaron		Exodus	84
Spy out the land	Caleb	1250-1200 BCE	Numbers	86
End of an era	Joshua		Deuteronomy	88
Spies sent to Jericho	Rahab		Joshua	91
The battle for Jericho	Joshua		Joshua	92
Joshua is tricked	Joshua		Joshua	94
Goodbye Joshua	Joshua		Joshua	96
CHAPTER 6 *Learning God's way* From the Bible books of Exodus, Leviticus, Numbers, and Deuteronomy				**97**
The holy meeting tent	Moses		Exodus	99
Inside God's tent	Moses		Exodus	100
Sacrifices for God	Moses	1200-1000 BCE	Exodus	102
Special clothes	Aaron		Exodus	104
Everybody is involved	12 tribes of Israel		Numbers	106
The Ten Commandments	Moses		Exodus	108
Freedom and justice for all	Moses		Leviticus	110
Laws to live by			Leviticus	112

Contents

Contents	Bible Characters	Period	Bible books	Page

CHAPTER 7 *The judges and Samson*
From the Bible books of Numbers, Judges, and Samuel — **113**

Contents	Bible Characters	Period	Bible books	Page
Balaam's talking donkey	Balaam		Numbers	114
Balaam listens to the donkey	Balaam		Numbers	116
After Joshua	Deborah, Barak	1200–1000 BCE	Judges	118
A brave woman	Jael, Sisera		Judges	120
Strange maths	Gideon		Judges	122
God calls a child	Hannah, Samuel		Samuel	124
Samson the strongest	Samson		Judges	126
Samson defeated	Delilah		Judges	128

CHAPTER 8 *David takes on Goliath*
From the Bible books of Ruth, 1 Samuel, 2 Samuel, 1 Kings and 2 Kings — **129**

Contents	Bible Characters	Period	Bible books	Page
The story of Ruth	Ruth		Ruth	130
Boaz marries Ruth	Boaz		Ruth	132
David takes on the giant	David, Goliath	1000–900 BCE	1 Samuel	134
Israel's first king	Saul		1 Samuel	136
David: Israel's greatest king	Bathsheba, Mephibosheth		2 Samuel	138
King Solomon	Solomon, Queen of Sheba		1 Kings	141
The dynamic duo	Elijah, Elisha		1 and 2 Kings	142
General Naaman's illness	Naaman, Elisha		2 Kings	144

Contents	Bible Characters	Period	Bible books	Page

10

CHAPTER 9 *Praising through problems*
From the Bible books of Esther, Job, and Psalms — **145**

	Bible Characters	Period	Bible books	Page
Esther saves the Jews	Esther	450 BCE	Esther	146
Job's suffering	Job		Job	148
Elihu's advice	Elihu		Job	150
Psalm 23	David	1000–900 BCE	Psalms	153
Thanking God for . . .			Psalms	154
Prayers for every kind of mood	David		Psalms	156
Learning from the Psalms			Psalms	158
Songs of praise			Psalms	160

CHAPTER 10 *Stunning words of wisdom*
From the Bible books of Proverbs, Ecclesiastes, and the Song of Solomon — **161**

	Bible Characters	Period	Bible books	Page
Proverbs galore	Solomon		Proverbs	162
All kinds of wisdom	Solomon		Proverbs	164
Nuggets of wisdom	Solomon		Proverbs	166
Spot the difference	Solomon	1000–900 BCE	Proverbs	168
More helpful advice	Solomon		Proverbs	170
Self-control	Solomon		Proverbs	172
What makes you happy?			Ecclesiastes	174
A time, a place for everything			Ecclesiastes	175
In love	Solomon		Song of Solomon	176

Contents	Bible Characters	Period	Bible books	Page
CHAPTER 11 *Isaiah's message of hope* From the Bible book of Isaiah				**177**
"Look out, Jerusalem!"	Isaiah		Isaiah	178
My vineyeard	Isaiah		Isaiah	179
Remember Israel	Isaiah		Isaiah	180
Other nations beware	Isaiah	800–700 BCE	Isaiah	182
Babylon	Isaiah		Isaiah	183
"Don't be so proud!"	Isaiah		Isaiah	184
Future hope	Isaiah		Isaiah	187
Hope in days of disaster	Isaiah		Isaiah	188
No peace for the wicked	Isaiah		Isaiah	190
Peace will dawn	Isaiah		Isaiah	192
CHAPTER 12 *Jeremiah's prophecies* From the Bible books of Jeremiah and Lamentations				**193**
God calls Jeremiah	Jeremiah		Jeremiah	194
God warns Jerusalem	Jeremiah		Jeremiah	196
The broken jar	Jeremiah	700–600 BCE	Jeremiah	198
Two baskets of figs	Jeremiah		Jeremiah	199
Jeremiah's unpopular message	Zedekiah		Jeremiah	200
Was Jeremiah a traitor?	Baruch, Jehudi		Jeremiah	202
Into the well	Ebed-Melech		Jeremiah	204

Contents	Bible Characters	Period	Bible books	Page
The is still hope	Jeremiah	700-600 BCE	Jeremiah	206
Jerusalem falls	Zedekiah		Jeremiah	207
Crying over Jerusalem	Nebuchadnezzar		Lamentations	208

CHAPTER 13 *Daniel with the lions*
From the Bible books of Ezekiel and Daniel **209**

Model-making	Ezekiel	600-500 BCE	Ezekiel	210
Acting it out	Ezekiel		Ezekiel	212
Is God fair?	Ezekiel		Ezekiel	214
Two lion cubs	Ezekiel		Ezekiel	215
The great crocodile	Ezekiel		Ezekiel	216
Two messages	Ezekiel		Ezekiel	218
Bones, bones, bones!	Ezekiel		Ezekiel	220
Can bones come alive?	Ezekiel		Ezekiel	221
Daniel in exile	Shadrach, Meshach, Abednego		Daniel	222
A night with the lions	Daniel		Daniel	224

CHAPTER 14 *Jonah's fishy tale*
From the Bible books of Hosea, Amos, Micah, Jonah, Obediah, Habakkuk, Zechariah and Malachi **225**

Two messages from Hosea	Hosea	800-400 BCE	Hosea	226
Insects invade	Joel		Joel	228
Amos speaks up against Israel	Amos		Amos	230

Contents	Bible Characters	Period	Bible books	Page
Jonah is rescued	Jonah		Jonah	232
Micah and war	Micah		Micah	234
Habakkuk's question	Habakkuk	800-400 BCE	Habakkuk	236
Zechariah's vision of a stone	Zechariah		Zechariah	238
Blessed by God	Malachi		Malachi	240

NEW TESTAMENT

CHAPTER 15 *Jesus the healer*
From the Bible books of Matthew, Mark and Luke   *241*

	Bible Characters	Period	Bible books	Page
Two babies to be born	Elizabeth, Mary		Luke	242
Jesus is born	Jesus (Mary, Joseph)		Luke	243
The child, Jesus	Jesus (Simeon, Anna)		Luke	244
The baptism of Jesus	Jesus (John the Baptist)		Matthew	245
Four fishers	Andrew, Peter, James, John	5 BCE-30 CE	Mark	246
The followers of Jesus	Simon, Andrew, James, John, Philip, Bartholomew, Thomas, Matthew, James, Thaddaeus, Simon, Judas		Matthew	247
The farmer and the seed	Jesus		Mark	248
A man with a crippled hand	Jesus		Mark	250
Jesus heals two men	Jesus		Matthew	251
Jesus heals a woman	Jesus		Mark	252

13

Contents	Bible Characters	Period	Bible books	Page
Jesus brings a girl back to life	Jairus	5 BCE–30 CE	Matthew	254
Mary and Martha	Mary, Martha		Luke	255
Everything changes	Jesus		Mark	256

14

CHAPTER 16 *Jesus is betrayed*
From the Bible books of Matthew, John and Acts **257**

Contents	Bible Characters	Period	Bible books	Page
One lost sheep	Jesus		Matthew	258
One lost coin	Jesus		Luke	259
The "whoevers"	Jesus		Matthew	260
Jesus is like a vine	Jesus		John	261
The special meal	Jesus		Matthew	262
Judas the betrayer	Judas Iscariot	5 BCE–50 CE	John	263
Jesus dies, but comes back to life	Joseph of Arimathea, Nicodemus, Mary Magdalene		John	264
The Holy Spirit comes			Acts	266
Peter and the cripple	Peter and John		Acts	267
The first Christian martyr	Stephen		Acts	268
Philip and the Ethiopian	Philip		Acts	270
Peter and Dorcas	Peter, Dorcas		Acts	271
Living for God	Writing of Romans		Romans	272

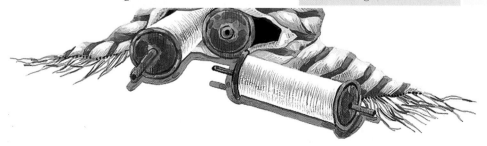

Contents	Bible Characters	Period	Bible books	Page
CHAPTER 17 *Paul's tough letters* From the Bible books of Romans, 1 Corinthians, 2 Corinthians, Galatians, Ephesians, Philippians, Colossians, and Thessalonians				**273**
A right telling off	Writing of 1 Corinthians		1 Corinthians	274
"How you boast!"	Writing of 1 Corinthians		1 Corinthians	275
New ways to live	Writing of 1 Corinthians		1 Corinthians	276
Paul's tough letter	Writing of Galatians		Galatians	278
Two ways	Writing of Galatians	50-60 CE	Galatians	280
Paul writes to the Ephesians	Writing of Ephesians		Ephesians	282
Advice to the Christians at Philippi	Writing of Philippians		Philippians	284
Paul's letter to the Colossians	Writing of Colossians		Colossians	285
Paul's first letter to the Christians at Thessalonica	Writing of 1 Thessalonians		1 Thessalonians	286
Jesus will return	Writing of 1 Thessalonians		1 Thessalonians	288
CHAPTER 18 *Paul's tender letters* From the Bible books of 2 Thessalonians, 1 Timothy, 2 Timothy, Titus, Philemon and James				**289**
"Keep working"	Writing of 2 Thessalonians		2 Thessalonians	290
Letters to Timothy	Paul, Timothy		1 Timothy	292
More advice for the church	Paul, Timothy	50-60 CE	1 Timothy	294
Timid Timothy	Writing of 2 Timothy		2 Timothy	296
The Scriptures	Writing of 2 Timothy		2 Timothy	298
Final words	Writing of 2 Timothy		2 Timothy	299

Contents	Bible Characters	Period	Bible books	Page

A letter to Titus	Writing of Titus		Titus	300
Philemon	Writing of Philemon	50-60 CE	Philemon	301
Teaching from James	Writing of James		James	302
Watch your tongue	Writing of James		James	304

CHAPTER 19 *Secrets from the book of Revelation*
From the Bible books of 2 Peter, 1 John, and Revelation **305**

Adding to your faith	Writing of 2 Peter		2 Peter	306
Walking in the light	Writing of 1 John		1 John	308
Good and evil	Writing of 1 John		1 John	310
The church in Ephesus	Writing of Revelation	60-100 CE	Revelation	312
The church in Smyrna	Writing of Revelation		Revelation	314
The church in Pergamum	Writing of Revelation		Revelation	316
The church in Laodicea	Writing of Revelation		Revelation	318
New heaven and earth	Writing of Revelation		Revelation	320

Chapter 1: From the Bible book of Genesis

Noah and the Great Flood

INTRODUCTION

This book begins at the beginning, with God creating the whole world, including us humans — made to be just like God.

As well as beauty, there is drama and sadness in the garden of Eden that God created.

The first murder is not hushed up.

Then comes God's rescue of Noah, his family and thousands of creatures from a great flood.

The story of the world's first disastrous building project, the uncompleted tower of Babel, follows.

Abraham, a great person of faith, is introduced. Although Abraham is elderly and childless, God promises that he will found a great nation.

The story of Lot's wife being turned into a pillar of salt is also included, along with the story of Abraham's first son, Ishmael, child of Hagar.

In the beginning

CREATOR GOD

In the beginning, God made heaven and earth. God breathed a wind over the deep emptiness. God made the light and called it day.

God made the darkness and called it night.

God made water, and God made the sky.

God made the ground and all its trees and plants, as well as all the vegetables and fruits.

God made the sun and the moon, the twinkling stars, and the animals, birds, fish and insects.

"IT WAS VERY GOOD"
God made people to be just like
God.

Everything that God created
was very good. God put Adam
and Eve in a wonderful garden.

**A river flows out of Eden
to water the garden.**
Genesis 2:10

The day the world changed

20

"So you can't eat the fruit on the trees?" murmured a snake to Eve.

"We can," Eve said. "But not the fruit on the tree giving knowledge of good and evil. God says if we eat that, we'll die."

"God's lying," hissed the snake. "You won't die. You'll be clever like God."

Eve ate the mouth-watering fruit and gave some to Adam.

It was true that the tree gave Adam and Eve knowledge. But God was angry at all of them. Adam and Eve had to leave the garden, but first, God made clothes for them.

God made garments of skins for the man and for his wife, and clothed them.

Genesis 3.21

MURDER

"I can't stand him. I'll kill him."

Eve's eldest son, Cain, a farmer, was jealous of his brother Abel.

One day, Cain killed his brother and buried his body.

"Where's Abel?" asked God.

"Search me. Am I my brother's keeper?"

"Abel's blood fell on the ground," said God. "Now nothing will grow for you."

So Cain had to leave.

He wandered far away from God.

Cain rose up against his brother Abel and killed him.

Genesis 4:8

Rain into rainbow

RAIN, RAIN, RAIN

God told Noah to build an ark. When the rains came, Noah and all his family went into the ark. With them, they took two of every creature on earth.

It seemed to rain for years.

Then it stopped.

Noah sent out a dove to see if the water had gone down. But the dove couldn't find any trees or ground to land on. It returned to the ark and landed on Noah's outstretched hand. Noah brought the dove into the ark.

Flood warnings

All over the world native peoples have passed down tales of a terrible flood. In one story the gods decided to drown the world because there was so much noise that they could not sleep. In another, the Epic of Gilgamesh, a man called Uta-Napishtim tells how the gods instructed him to build a boat to escape a flood. Like Noah, he sent out birds to check if the water had gone down.

Many scholars believe that the stories may be based on memories of an actual worldwide flood that took place at the end of the last Ice Age — the flood described in the Bible.

23

The flood continued for forty days on the earth . . . and bore up the ark, and it rose high above the earth.

Genesis 7:17

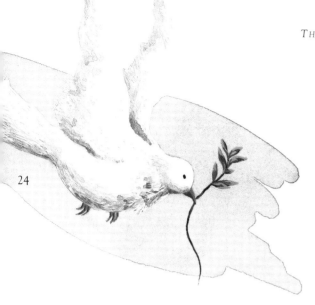

24

*[God said] "As long as
the earth endures,
seedtime and harvest,
cold and heat, summer
and winter, day and
night, shall not cease."*

Genesis 8:22

A week later Noah sent off the dove again. The dove
flew back. It had a freshly picked olive leaf in its beak.
Yes — the floods were going down at last.

Noah waited another week and sent the dove out
again. It never came back.

"There must be dry land around," thought Noah.

RAINBOW

"Come out of the ark now, Noah," God said.

So out they came — from the tiniest ant to the
largest elephant.

And, in the sky, a most magnificent rainbow
greeted them. "This rainbow is a sign of my promises

to you and to all the earth," God explained. All of
Noah's family looked at the dazzling colours in the
rainbow and knew that God loved them.

25

*"Bring out with you
every living thing . . .
birds and animals and
every creeping thing."*

Genesis 8:17

The tower of Babel

> *"Come, let us build*
> *ourselves a city, and*
> *a tower."*
>
> Genesis 11:4

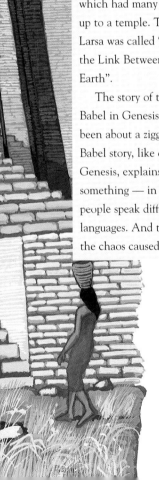

Ziggurats

Cities in Mesopotamia often had a tower called a "ziggurat", which had many steps leading up to a temple. The ziggurat at Larsa was called "The House of the Link Between Heaven and Earth".

The story of the tower of Babel in Genesis may have been about a ziggurat. The Babel story, like others in Genesis, explains what caused something — in this case, why people speak different languages. And the story shows the chaos caused by pride.

A TALL STORY

"Let's make a name for ourselves," said the people who lived by the Euphrates River.

"How?"

"We'll build a tower with a top that touches the sky. We'll be famous. No one will be able to put a stop to us or split us up."

DANGEROUS TALK

God saw what they were doing. "If they carry on like this, they'll think they can do anything," God said.

So God muddled up their one language into a babble of different languages.

"Talk sense," each one said, "I can't understand a word you're saying."

Work on the tower stopped, and the people drifted away to live in other places.

28

Into the unknown

Abram took his wife Sarai and his brother's son Lot.

Genesis 12:5

Now there was a famine in the land. So Abram went down to Egypt.

Genesis 12:10

Abraham lived in Haran, where everyone worshipped the moon. One day God said, "Leave this place, and go to the land I'll show you."

So Abraham set out, with his wife Sarah, and his nephew Lot.

They travelled hundreds of miles. At last, in the south of Canaan, God said, "You've arrived. Look around. I'm giving all this land to you and your descendants." And Abraham believed God.

Genesis chapter 12 verses 1 to 20 and chapter 15 verses 1 to 6

"Look towards heaven and count the stars, if you are able."

Genesis 15:5

LIAR!

Famine! Abraham set off again, through the wilderness to Egypt.

Now Sarah was beautiful and Abraham was scared. He said, "Some Egyptian will murder me to marry you. Say you're my sister."

Pharaoh fell in love with Sarah. He gave Abraham sheep, cattle, camels, donkeys and servants. Abraham took them all, and Pharaoh took Sarah. When Pharaoh found out the truth he threw Abraham, Sarah and Lot out of the country. Egyptians hated liars.

THE STARS

Back in Canaan, God spoke to Abraham. "Look at the stars. Count them if you can. I'll give you as many descendants as there are stars." And Abraham believed God.

A city in flames

Abraham's nephew Lot made a serious error. He went off to live in the city of Sodom, to the south of the Dead Sea.

Sodom was a vile, evil city.

One evening, Lot was sitting by the city gates when he saw two strangers. They were angels, but Lot didn't know that. He did know that it wasn't safe to be out in Sodom after dark.

"Come and stay at my house," Lot said.

That night the angels said, "This city will be destroyed. As soon as it's light, get away with your family. Run for your lives. And don't look back."

Lot's wife, behind him, looked back, and she became a pillar of salt.

Genesis 19:26

As Lot was escaping with his wife and two daughters he heard a great roaring sound. The ground was shaking. There was a terrible smell.

Lot's wife couldn't stop herself. She turned round. The delay was fatal.

Genesis chapter 21 verses 1 to 21

Ismael is looked after

32

Ishmael was Abraham's first child. His pride and joy.

Ishmael's mother, Hagar, was a slave. She belonged to Sarah, who was Abraham's wife. Sarah was childless, so she gave Hagar to her husband as a second wife (that was the custom in those days).

Later, Sarah had a baby, Isaac.

"Spoilt brat!" thought Ishmael and made fun of Isaac.

"Throw that slave and her child out!" shouted Sarah.

"Do as Sarah says," God said.

Hagar and Ishmael wandered in the desert till their water was gone and they collapsed. Then Hagar heard a voice, an angel. "God has heard the boy crying," the angel said. He led them to a well.

God was with Ishmael and he grew up to be a great desert warrior.

Name Change
God changed Abram's name to Abraham and Sarai's name to Sarah (Genesis 17:5, 15) as a sign of God's promises to them.

So Abraham rose early in the morning, and took bread, and a skin of water, and gave it to Hagar.

Genesis 21:14

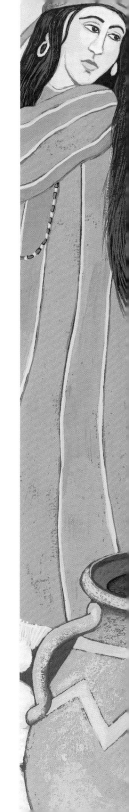

Chapter 2: From the Bible book of Genesis

Abraham's amazing faith

INTRODUCTION

This book starts with God ordering Abraham to sacrifice his much loved son, Isaac.

Abraham's servant is then sent on a seemingly impossible mission to find a girl, whose name and address he does not know. And the girl must be prepared to become Isaac's bride without even meeting him.

The story of God's love for God's people, the Israelites, then focuses on cheats.

Jacob cheats elder brother Esau out of his birthright.

Jacob is helped in all this by their scheming mother, Rebekah.

Then the cheat, Jacob, is outwitted by his ever-so-cunning uncle, Laban.

Yet through all this God promises to be with Jacob, to protect Jacob and to make a great nation of his descendants.

God's test for Abraham

34

THE KNIFE IS POISED

Abraham was an old man when he and his wife, Sarah, had a child.

Now God told Abraham to take his son, Isaac, and sacrifice him!

Abraham cut the wood to burn the sacrifice. He gave the wood to Isaac to carry. Abraham had the fire and a very sharp knife.

Isaac asked his father the burning question: "I see the fire and the wood, but where is the lamb for the sacrifice?"

Genesis chapter 22 verses 1 to 19

Abraham calmly replied, "God will provide the sacrifice, my son."

Then Abraham built an altar, arranged the wood on it, tied up Isaac, and put him on top of the wood. Abraham took a firm grip on his gleaming knife, raised his hand to . . .

A RAM TO THE RESCUE

. . . when he heard a voice ringing in his ears.

It was God's angel calling him. "Abraham! Abraham!"

Abraham froze. "I'm here," he replied.

"Don't lay a finger on the boy," the angel instructed.

"I know for sure that you fear God, as you would have given God your only son."

Then Abraham looked up.

God had provided the sacrifice.

There, caught in a bush by his horns, was a ram.

Abraham then sacrificed the ram instead of Isaac.

Isaac said to his father Abraham, "Father! . . . The fire and the wood are here, but where is the lamb for a burnt-offering?"

Genesis 22:7

A marriage made in heaven

A BRIDE FOR ISAAC

Abraham was now very old. His thoughts turned to the future. What would happen to God's followers after his death?

Abraham's son, Isaac, needed a wife, but she had to be an Israelite. Abraham turned to his trusted head servant.

"Swear by God," Abraham ordered his servant, "the God of heaven and earth, that you will not take a wife for my son from the daughters of the Canaanites. Go to my country and my people and find a bride for Isaac there."

"But," ventured the servant, "what if this woman refuses to come back with me?"

"That won't happen," said Abraham confidently. "God will send an angel ahead of you."

THE SERVANT PRAYED

So off the servant went, with ten of Abraham's camels laden with gifts. He arrived at a town called Nahor and his thirsty camels eyed the well, longingly.

The servant prayed: "God, may I be successful today. Please show your great love to Abraham in this way."

THE WATER TEST FOR REBEKAH

The servant prayed that if the girl who gave him water to drink also offered to water his camels, then she should be Isaac's bride.

*Before he had finished
speaking, there was
Rebekah . . . coming out
with her water-jar on
her shoulder.*

Genesis 24:15

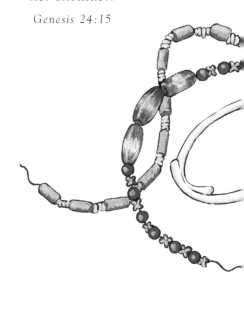

A successful mission

Camels watered

"Here is a drink for you, sir," said Rebekah politely to the servant. Then she emptied her water-jar into a trough for his ten camels.

That was it. Rebekah was the one. "Thank God for guiding me in this way," the servant prayed.

The servant then gave Rebekah a gold ring and two gold bracelets. He asked about her father, and if he could stay the night with her family.

Laban's welcome

Rebekah ran back home. She had so much to tell her mum, her dad Bethuel, and Laban, her brother. When Laban saw the ring and the bracelets, he ran out to the well.

"Come and stay with me," Laban said to Abraham's servant. "You're very welcome." Laban looked after the camels, giving them straw and water.

"REBEKAH IS YOURS"

Bethuel and Laban listened intently to the servant's story. They agreed to his wish.

"This is clearly from God," Bethuel and Laban concluded. "Rebekah is yours. Take her and return to Abraham. As God has said, Rebekah must marry your master's son."

So Rebekah returned with Abraham's servant. She met Isaac, who fell in love with her, and became his wife.

When she had finished giving him a drink, she said, "I will draw for your camels also."

Genesis 24:19

One happy family

The amazing thing about this story is that Abraham's servant went straight to the home of a family who were already related to Abraham.

Rebekah was the daughter of Bethuel.

Bethuel was the son of Milcah and Nahor.

Nahor was Abraham's brother.

So when Abraham's son, Isaac, married Rebekah, he was marrying his father's great-niece.

For Rebekah was the grand-daughter of Abraham's brother.

Rebekah's family tree

```
Abraham ————┴———— Nahor
   |                  |
 Isaac             Bethuel
                      |
                   Rebekah
```

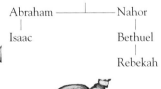

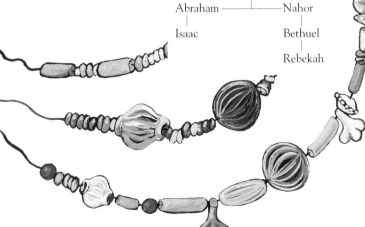

Nonidentical twins

ESAU AND JACOB

Isaac and Rebekah had twin sons.

The firstborn son was Esau and the second-born son was Jacob. But nobody would have guessed that they were twins.

Esau loved the open fields. He became a skilled hunter.

But Jacob was quieter — more of a stay-at-home type.

A BOWL OF SOUP

Jacob was jealous of Esau because he was the oldest.

One day Esau came home famished after hunting in the fields. His mouth watered as he smelled the lentil soup Jacob was stirring.

"I'm starving," announced Esau. "Let me have some of your soup."

"Okay," said cunning Jacob, "but only in exchange for your rights as the

first-born son."

"Okay, it's a deal. Just give me some of your red soup," responded Esau.

Esau gives away his birthright

The firstborn son
In those days, the firstborn son inherited twice as much from his father as the second son did. This was the "birthright" Esau traded away.

The blessing
In those days, people believed that a blessing released a power that could never be undone. Isaac couldn't take back the blessing that Jacob stole. This blessing would make Jacob the head of his people.

Once when Jacob was cooking a stew, Esau came in from the field . . . Esau said to Jacob, "Let me eat some of that red stuff, for I am famished!"

Genesis 25:29-30

More than a family squabble

REBEKAH'S PLAN

Jacob was his mum's (Rebekah's) favourite.

Esau was the apple of his dad's (Isaac's) eye.

Rebekah overheard the elderly, and nearly blind, Isaac having a quiet word with Esau.

"Esau, my son," Isaac said slowly, "take your bow and arrow, and go out into the country. Kill an animal, and prepare my favourite meal. I'll eat it and then give you my special blessing."

Rebekah went straight to Jacob with this news.

"Now, Jacob," schemed Rebekah, "do as I say, and the blessing will be yours."

So Jacob picked two fat young goats from the flock. Rebekah made them into a tasty dish — just the sort that she knew Isaac loved.

"I'M SMOOTH-SKINNED"

"Now, Jacob," whispered Rebekah, "this is your chance. Give this to your dad to eat."

"But," protested Jacob, "I'm smooth-skinned, while Esau is hairy. Dad may be half blind, but he'll know I'm not Esau when he touches me."

Quick as a flash, Rebekah said, "Don't worry. Put on these clothes — they're Esau's best, and wrap these goat skins around your hands and neck. They'll fool your dad."

The trick worked. Isaac thought Jacob was Esau and gave him his special blessing.

Genesis chapter 27 verses 1 to 29

"Cursed be everyone who curses you, and blessed be everyone who blesses you!"

Genesis 27:29

43

Jacob leaves home

44

ESCAPING FROM ESAU

When Esau found out about the trick Rebekah and Jacob had played on Isaac, he was mad with anger. He was out to kill Jacob.

And he dreamed that there was a ladder set up on the earth . . . and the angels of God were ascending and descending on it.

Genesis 28:12

Rebekah told Jacob, "Esau knows you cheated him out of his birthright and blessing. Now he's after your blood. Leave here and go to my brother, Laban, so Esau has time to cool down."

On his way to his Uncle Laban, Jacob spent the night at Bethel. He slept under the stars and used a stone as his pillow.

JACOB'S DREAM

That night Jacob had a dream he never forgot.

He saw angels going up and down a huge ladder. God stood above the ladder.

Then God spoke to Jacob:

"I am the God of Abraham, your grandfather; the God of Isaac, your father.

"I will give the land you are now asleep on to your descendants.

"They will be as many as the dust of the earth.

"I will be with you. I will protect you."

The cheat is cheated

So Jacob served seven years for Rachel, and they seemed to him but a few days because of the love he had for her.

Genesis 29:20

LEAH AND RACHEL

Jacob arrived at Laban's farm where he became a shepherd.

Laban had two daughters. The elder daughter, Leah, had lovely eyes, and the younger daughter, Rachel, was graceful and beautiful. Jacob fell in love with Rachel.

A SEVEN-YEAR-LONG ENGAGEMENT

Laban promised Jacob that he could marry his daughter Rachel. But first, Jacob had to work for him for seven years. Jacob loved Rachel so much that the seven years passed in a moment.

Genesis chapter 29 verses 1 to 30

Leah's eyes were lovely,
and Rachel was graceful
and beautiful.

Genesis 29:17

LABAN'S TRICK

After seven years, Jacob said to Laban, "Now I can marry Rachel."

So Laban laid on a great party. Then, in the evening, Laban gave Jacob one of his daughters. She was wearing a veil.

In the morning Jacob went to Laban, white-hot with anger:

"You gave me your daughter Leah. But I wanted Rachel!"

"Ah," replied Jacob, "we have a custom that the younger daughter can't marry before the older daughter is married.

"Work for me for seven more years and Rachel is yours."

Jacob had no option but to agree.

Rachel's theft

48

Rachel stole her father's household gods.

Genesis 31:19

HUNT THE IDOL

After Jacob's flocks of goats and sheep had become very numerous, God spoke to Jacob again:

"Jacob. Go back to the land where you were raised. I will be with you."

As they left, Rachel stole Laban's precious idols. Even though Laban came after Jacob, looking for his idols, he never found them. Rachel had hidden them in her camel's saddle.

FRIENDS AGAIN

Jacob was terrified to see Esau again, but Esau ran to meet him, crying with joy.

Chapter 3: From the Bible book of Genesis

Joseph's startling dreams

INTRODUCTION

This chapter is all about the life of Joseph.

It starts with a teenager having two startling dreams.

Joseph's life takes an unpromising turn when he is thrown into a dry well by his brothers. Then he becomes a slave in Egypt.

Joseph's see-saw life takes a turn for the better when he is put in charge of the home of Potiphar, a very important Egyptian soldier.

Next, a bizarre twist of events lands Joseph in prison.

Who could have guessed that he would then become vice president of Egypt, save the Egyptians from a seven-year famine, and arrange for his father and brothers to live with him in Egypt?

Joseph the dreamer

50

DAD'S FAVOURITE SON

Joseph, Jacob's favourite son, worked with his brothers as a shepherd. Once, when he was 17, he gave his father a bad report about his brothers. The brothers were furious. Then, to show how much he loved Joseph, Jacob gave him a special robe with long sleeves. The brothers were green with envy.

Joseph's coat

What did it look like?
The coat which Jacob made for Joseph is popularly known as Joseph's "coat of many colours." This comes from the translation of this verse in the King James Version of the Bible.

Instead of colours, the robe may have had stripes, patterns, or long sleeves.

What did it mean?
The robe was a mark of Jacob's favouritism for the son he loved best.

This coat may have shown that Jacob planned to leave his wealth to Joseph after he died.

SHEAVES

One morning, Joseph told his brothers about a dream he'd just had.

"We were in the field tying up bundles of wheat. Then my bundle stood up and your eleven bundles of wheat gathered around mine. Then your bundles bowed to my bundle."

"So you think you're going to be a king and rule over us," mocked his brothers.

He [Joseph] said to them, "Listen to this dream that I dreamed. There we were, binding sheaves in the field . . . Your sheaves . . . bowed down to my sheaf."

Genesis 37:6-7

Dreams don't seem to come true

52

*"Look, I have had
another dream: the sun,
the moon, and eleven
stars were bowing down
to me."*

Genesis 37:9

THE STARS

Joseph had another dream. This was the last straw.

This time, Joseph told his brothers, "The sun, the moon, and eleven stars were all bowing down to me."

When Joseph told his father, Jacob told him off, saying, "Do you expect your mother and me, along with your brothers, to bow down to you?"

Worst of all, the brothers hated Joseph even more because Jacob took such notice of Joseph's dream.

INTO A WELL

Jacob told Joseph to check on his brothers, who had gone to Shechem with flocks of sheep.

Joseph found them at Dothan. But they saw him coming and hatched a plot.

"Let's kill him. We'll tell Dad that a bear killed him," they schemed.

"No," said the oldest brother, Reuben, "don't hurt him. Just throw him into this empty well."

So into the well went Joseph.

When Reuben left, the other brothers sold Joseph to some Ishmaelite traders.

Genesis chapter 37 verses 25 to 36 and chapter 39 verses 1 to 20

Sold into slavery

55

Jacob mourns for Joseph

Tearing clothes

When Jacob thought that Joseph had been killed by a wild animal he tore his clothes. When Reuben found that Joseph had been taken out of the well he tore his clothes. This was a sign of deep sorrow.

Wearing sackcloth

Another way to express sadness over someone's death in those days was to wear coarse and uncomfortable sackcloth instead of normal clothes.

They . . . sold him to the Ishmaelites for twenty pieces of silver.

Genesis 37:28

JACOB'S SADNESS

When the brothers returned to Jacob they showed him Joseph's special robe. They had stripped him of it and dipped it in goat's blood.

"Yes, Dad. Isn't it sad. Some wild animal obviously killed Joseph," the brothers lied.

Jacob tore his clothes and dressed in sackcloth. He was so sad that nothing and nobody could comfort him. "I'll be overcome with sadness until my dying day," said Jacob.

POTIPHAR

The Ishmaelite traders took Joseph to Egypt and sold him to an important soldier called Potiphar, who was captain of the palace guard.

All would have been fine for Joseph but for Potiphar's wife. Because Joseph refused her advances, Potiphar's wife lied about him and Potiphar threw Joseph into prison.

Joseph in prison

56

*"I also had a dream:
there were three cake
baskets on my head."*

Genesis 40:16

THE WINE WAITER'S DREAM

In prison Joseph knew that God was with him and still looking after him.

Even the prison warden liked Joseph, and he was put in charge of the other prisoners.

The king's wine waiter was also in prison and told Joseph about a dream he had.

"I saw a vine which had three branches. I squeezed juice from its grapes into the king's cup," recounted the wine waiter.

"This means," explained Joseph, "that in three days you will be freed."

"And when you're free, remember me. Tell the king about me so I will be freed as well," added Joseph.

THE BAKER'S DREAM

Then the king's baker, who was also in prison, told Joseph his dream.

"On my head, I saw three baskets and birds ate food from the top basket," said the baker, hopefully.

57

"In three days' time," Joseph told him, "the king
will kill you and birds will eat you."

Both these dreams came true, exactly as Joseph had
said. But no one helped Joseph to be released from
prison.

THE KING'S DREAM

Two years later, unknown to Joseph, the king also had
a dream. It was all about seven skinny cows gobbling
up seven fat cows!

*And there came up out
of the Nile seven sleek
and fat cows . . . Then
seven other cows, ugly
and thin, came up out of
the Nile after them.*

Genesis 41:2-3

A prisoner advises a king

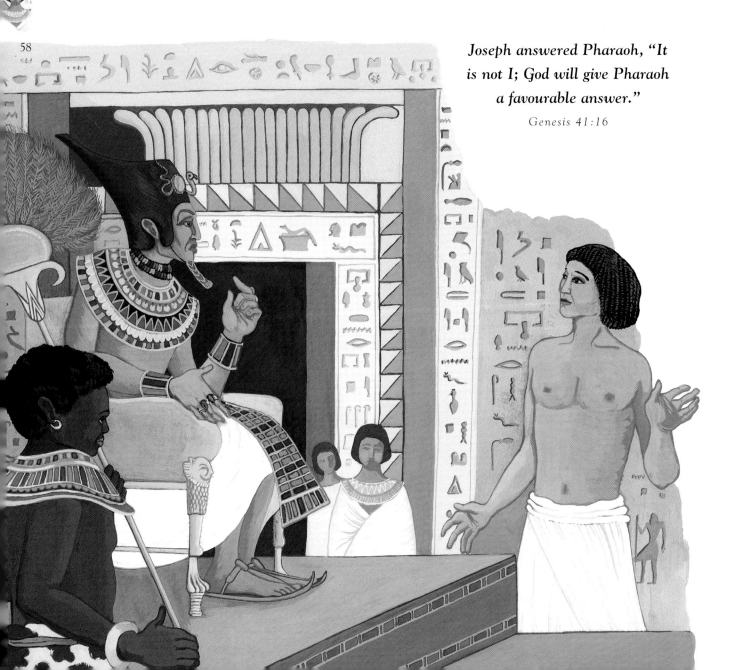

Joseph answered Pharaoh, "It is not I; God will give Pharaoh a favourable answer."

Genesis 41:16

THE KING'S SECOND DREAM

The following night the king had another dream.

He saw seven good heads of grain on one stalk. Then he saw seven thin and shrivelled heads of grain. The thin grain gobbled up the good grain.

"Come on now," bellowed the king to his magicians and wise advisors. "I've told you my dreams. You tell me what they mean!"

The silence was deafening. Nobody could interpret the king's dreams.

THE WINE WAITER REMEMBERS

"Your majesty," said the wine waiter hesitantly, "when I was in prison the baker and I had dreams. A young Hebrew man told us what they meant."

"Send for that man," ordered the king.

BOTH DREAMS MEAN THE SAME THING

"The king's calling for you, Joseph," beamed the friendly prison guard. "You'd better have a quick wash, shave and change of clothes."

Joseph explained the dreams: Egypt was going to have seven years of great harvests followed by seven years when nothing would grow.

Joseph's brothers come to Egypt

60

JOSEPH BECOMES VICE PRESIDENT

The king made Joseph the second most powerful person in the land. He put Joseph in charge of organizing everything so that there would be enough food to last during the seven bad harvests.

"Here you are, Joseph. Here's my special ring with my own personal royal seal on it.

"Here's a set of best linen clothes for you to wear.

"And here's a gold chain for you.

"And here's the second best chariot in the land for you to ride in."

A DREAM COMES TRUE

Ten men came before Joseph. They didn't recognize Joseph, but Joseph knew that they were ten of his eleven brothers. They bowed before him, just like the sheaves and stars had done in his dreams.

"We've come all the way from Canaan to buy food, sir," the men pleaded.

Joseph pretended not to know them. Then he ordered them to return to their homeland and bring back the one missing brother, whose name was Benjamin. Joseph put Simeon in prison as a hostage.

When Joseph came
home, they brought him
the present . . . and
bowed to the ground
before him.

Genesis 43:26

Joseph and his brothers

62

ELEVEN BROTHERS GO TO EGYPT

The nine brothers returned with sacks of grain to Canaan, and, with great difficulty, persuaded their father Jacob to allow Benjamin to return with them to Joseph.

JOSEPH'S TRAP

Joseph pretended to allow the eleven brothers to return home a second time, laden with as much grain as they could carry.

He had secretly told one of his servants to put his silver cup in Benjamin's sack.

After they had left for Canaan Joseph sent a servant after them.

He searched, beginning with the eldest and ending with the youngest; and the cup was found in Benjamin's sack.

Genesis 44:12

63

"Whoever has stolen my master's silver cup will be his slave," the servant threatened.

The cup was, of course, found in Benjamin's sack.

"Please, sir," pleaded the brothers, "let Benjamin return home. Or else it will break his father's heart."

JOSEPH SAYS WHO HE IS

With only his brothers in the room, Joseph then broke down and wept.

He told his eleven brothers, "I am your brother, Joseph."

The eleven brothers were stunned.

Then they hugged each other with joy and amazement.

Then he fell upon his brother Benjamin's neck and wept, while Benjamin wept.

Genesis 45:14

Genesis chapter 45 verse 9 to chapter 49 verse 28

Jacob goes to Egypt

64

Joseph told his eleven brothers to go back to Jacob, who was also called Israel. "Tell him all that has happened to me — how I'm now vice president of Egypt. I'll look after you all during the next five years of the famine," promised Joseph.

Jacob was pleased to hear this unbelievably good news. He said, "I'm going to go to Egypt to see Joseph before I die."

WELCOME JACOB

When the king of Egypt heard about Joseph's brothers, he gave them the best of everything in Egypt.

When Jacob arrived, Joseph and Jacob hugged each other. Joseph brought his two sons to meet the grandfather they had never seen.

Jacob put his hands gently on the heads of Joseph's sons, and blessed them.

Joseph said to his father, "They are my sons . . ." And he said, "Bring them to me, please, that I may bless them."

Genesis 48:9

Chapter 4: From the Bible book of Exodus

Moses and the great escape

INTRODUCTION

This chapter tells the gripping story of the Israelites escaping from Egypt.

It is told through the eyes of Moses. Many remarkable things happened to him in his life. To start with, his survival as a baby was against all the odds. That's because the king of Egypt had commanded that all baby boys born to the Israelites should be thrown into the River Nile.

Then Moses had the never-to-be-forgotten experience in the desert of seeing a burning bush that somehow did not burn up.

Moses was given the thankless task of tackling the king of Egypt. Each time the king refused to let the Israelites go, God sent a plague to devastate the Egyptians.

The dramatic climax of the escape from Egypt comes in the parting of the waters of the Red Sea.

The Israelites grow

*The daughter of Pharaoh
came down to bathe at
the river . . . she saw
the child. He was crying,
and she took pity on him.*

Exodus 2:5,6

Exodus chapter 1 verse 1 to chapter 2 verse 10

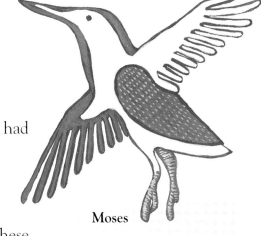

FROM 70 PEOPLE TO A GREAT NATION

When Jacob arrived in Egypt, his eleven sons and their families were 70 people. The people of Israel had many children and their number grew.

A NEW KING OF EGYPT

When a new king began to rule Egypt, he said, "These Israelites are going to overrun us. Kill all their baby boys! Throw them into the River Nile."

MOSES IS BORN

The brave Hebrew midwives refused to do what the king commanded. One Israelite mother hid her baby boy in a basket among the tall reeds of the River Nile. Miriam, Moses' sister, watched over him. The king's daughter discovered him, felt sorry for him, and adopted him as her own son.

Moses

What does "Moses" mean?

"Moses", an Egyptian name, means "is born".

The king's daughter explained that she called the baby "Moses" because she "drew him out of the water" (Exodus 2:10). This is a word play as "Moses" sounds like the Hebrew word for "draw out".

Just as Moses was rescued from the Nile, so God delivered the people from the Red Sea.

Moses runs away from Egypt

MOSES SUPPORTS HIS PEOPLE

Moses grew up in the king's palace, but he loved his own people, the Israelites. He couldn't stand the way the Egyptians forced them to work as slaves and treated them so cruelly. One day Moses saw an Israelite being beaten, so he killed the Egyptian and hid his body in the sand. But news about this soon spread. Moses ran for his life.

THE BURNING BUSH

One day Moses saw flames of fire coming out of a bush. But the bush wasn't burned up. Moses said, "I must take a closer look at this. How can a bush have flames and not be burned?"

RESCUE MISSION

Then God spoke to Moses from the bush,

"Moses, Moses! Take off your sandals.

"You are standing on holy ground.

"I am the God of Abraham, the God of Isaac and the God of Jacob.

"My people, the Israelites, are slaves. I now order you to go to the king of Egypt and tell him to let my people go."

Exodus chapter 2 verse 11 to chapter 3 verse 10

Then Moses said, "I
must turn aside and look
at this great sight, and
see why the bush is not
burned up."

Exodus 3:3

"Let my people go"

*But Pharaoh said,
"Who is the LORD, that
I should heed him
and let Israel go?"*

Exodus 5:2

Moses could not believe his ears. "I'm no great man. How can I possibly go to the king of Egypt and lead the people out of Egypt?" Moses protested.

God replied, "I will be with you to help you do this. You will lead the people out of Egypt. Then you will all worship me on this mountain."

Read-the-story-for-yourself
....
Exodus chapter 3 verse 11 to chapter 5 verse 21

71

Aaron speaks for Moses

"Please, God," Moses said, "can't you send someone else to do this. I'm not even good at speaking."

"Your brother, Aaron, can speak for you. You tell him what I tell you, and Aaron will speak to the king," God replied.

"Let my people go"

Moses and Aaron went to the king of Egypt. They said to him, "This is what the God of Israel says, 'Let my people go, so they can hold a festival for me in the desert.'"

The king is not amused

"How dare you stop the slaves from working!" raged the king.

"Don't give the people any more straw to make the bricks with," the king ordered the slave masters. "But make sure they still make as many bricks."

"That'll teach them," the king thought to himself.

But the king of Egypt said to them, "Moses and Aaron, why are you taking the people away from their work?"

Exodus 5:4

Miserable Moses

The Israelites were fed up with Moses for landing them with such extra work.

Moses was fed up with God. "Look what trouble you've brought on us," Moses complained.

"Don't worry," replied God. "I will use my great power and the king of Egypt will let my people go."

Exodus chapter 5 verse 22 to chapter 8 verse 15

And the frogs came
up and covered the
land of Egypt.

Exodus 8:6

73

PLAGUE NUMBER ONE: WATER TURNS TO BLOOD

"I will punish the Egyptians in terrible ways," God promised.

"Tell Aaron," said God, "to stretch out his staff over the rivers, ponds, canals and pools of Egypt." Every drop of water was turned into blood.

PLAGUE NUMBER TWO: FROGS

"Tell the king that the land will be filled with frogs if he does not let my people go," said God.

The frogs went everywhere: in the king's palace, under the beds, in the ovens, behind the saucepans, on the sandals — one even sat on the king's throne!

*. . . and the fish in the
river died. The river
stank so that the
Egyptians could not
drink its water, and
there was blood
throughout the whole
land of Egypt.*

Exodus 7:21

Plagues galore!

PLAGUES THREE TO NINE

There were ten plagues in all. The next were:

Plague number three: gnats

Plague number four: flies

Plague number five: disease on farm animals

Plague number six: boils

Plague number seven: hail

Plague number eight: locusts

Plague number nine: darkness

It caused festering boils on humans and animals.

Exodus 9:10

74

ONLY EGYPTIANS SUFFER

Each plague hit only the Egyptians. The worst
hailstorm in history destroyed everything in the
Egyptian fields. But in the land of Goshen, where the
Israelites lived, there were no hailstones.

THE KING'S STUBBORN HEART

As each plague ravaged the Egyptians, the king
acted in the same way.

When the plague of locusts
had gobbled up every leaf from
every plant on Egyptian
land, the king sent for
Moses and Aaron and said,
"Get rid of these locusts. I
promise I'll let you go. Only
get rid of the locusts."

As soon as the locusts
disappeared the king changed
his mind.

All the dust of the earth
turned into gnats
throughout the whole
land of Egypt.

Exodus 8:17

The last plague

THE TENTH PLAGUE

The tenth and final plague was the plague to end all plagues.

Moses told the king, "This is what God says: 'About midnight tonight I will go through all Egypt. Every firstborn son in the land of Egypt will die. The firstborn son of the king, who sits on his throne, will die. Even the firstborn of the slave girl grinding grain will die. Also the firstborn farm animals will die. There will be loud crying everywhere in Egypt. It will be worse than any time before or after this.'"

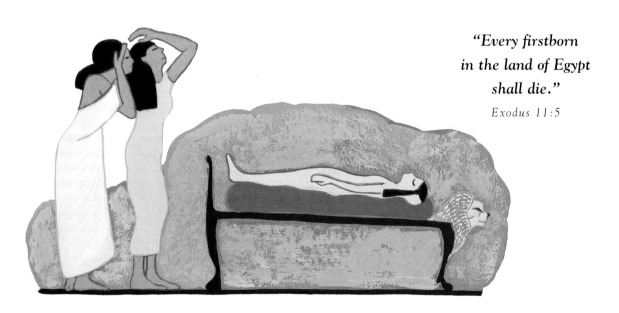

"Every firstborn in the land of Egypt shall die."

Exodus 11:5

Exodus chapters 11 and 12

A midnight to remember

A STUBBORN KING

Of course, Moses and Aaron knew what would happen. Aaron would warn the king about what God was about to do, but the king would be unmoved. The king had a stubborn hard heart. He would not let God's people leave his country.

That night, at midnight, it happened. Pharaoh woke up. There was the sound of loud crying across the whole land.

And he [Pharaoh] did not let the people of Israel go out of his land.

Exodus 11:10

The great escape

The king called Moses and Aaron in the middle of the night. "Get out of here," he commanded. "Take all the Israelites with you, and all your animals. Begone!" There were no signposts to help Moses lead the hundreds of thousands of God's people out of Egypt. God led them through the desert towards the Red Sea.

A PILLAR OF CLOUD AND A PILLAR OF FIRE

God guided Moses and showed him which way to take. During the day God went ahead of the Israelites in a pillar of cloud. During the night God was in a pillar of fire which threw light on the track to follow.

"RAISE YOUR STAFF"

Just as he had done before, the king changed his mind. Moses and God's people now had the Egyptian army advancing behind them and the Red Sea in front of them. Was this the end? Would it be a watery grave or would the soldiers in the king's 600 best chariots make mincemeat of them?

   Then it happened. As Moses raised his staff and held it over the sea, the sea split. There was a wall of water on both sides of them. But the Israelites went across on dry land.

The LORD went in front
of them in a pillar of
cloud by day . . . and in
a pillar of fire by night.

Exodus 13:21

Exodus chapter 14 verses 26 to 30, and chapter 15

Songs of praise

80

"WE'VE ESCAPED"

The Egyptian soldiers tried to follow the Israelites, but their chariot wheels stuck in the mud and the Egyptians could not escape when the walls of water closed in on them. It was a miracle the Israelites would never forget. They had escaped from Egypt. God had led them.

THE SONG OF MIRIAM AND MOSES

Moses and the Israelites sang to celebrate their escape:

"I will sing to God, who gives me strength. God has saved us; he has led us out of slavery in Egypt."

REACH FOR THE TAMBOURINES

This was a day for the tambourines. Miriam, Aaron's sister, banging her tambourine for all she was worth, led the women in their song of praise to God: "Sing to God, sing praises to God. God has thrown the army into the sea. We're free, we're free."

Then the prophet Miriam, Aaron's sister, took a tambourine in her hand.

Exodus 15:20

Chapter 5: From the Bible books of Exodus, Numbers, Deuteronomy and Joshua

God's people journey through the desert

INTRODUCTION

Life in the desert was certainly very different from being a slave in Egypt.

But Moses was faced with so many new problems. Where was there water to be found in the desert? What about food for 600,000 people every day? Then there was the constant grumbling and complaining of the Israelites. Worst of all, Moses even found them worshipping a golden calf.

Moses, who did not live to see the end of the journey, appointed Joshua to lead the people after he was dead.

Joshua sent spies into the land of Canaan, then led the people in battle to capture its cities, including the important city of Jericho.

Problems in the desert

Things did not go smoothly for Moses after he led God's people out of their slavery in Egypt.

NO FOOD

When their food ran out, the Israelites immediately blamed Moses. "Did you bring us out into this parched desert to die of hunger?" they said to Moses accusingly.

Moses told them that they were grumbling against God when they grumbled against him and Aaron.

"God will provide you with meat in the evenings.

"God will provide you with bread in the mornings," Moses assured the people.

Amazingly this happened. In the evening, tasty birds called quails flew in on the wind. They were easy to catch. In the mornings the people collected thin flakes like frost from the ground. "What's this?" they asked Moses.

"It's bread that God has given you to eat," replied Moses.

Quails

How did they arrive?
Quails are a small game bird and are considered to be a great delicacy.

Quails migrate in very large flocks. They are carried along by the prevailing winds.

How were quails caught?
Quails are not very good at flying. Often they travel only three or four feet above the ground.

82

NO WATER

Then the Israelites ran out of water. Once again they put the blame on Moses.

God told Moses to hit a rock at Mount Sinai with the same staff that he raised to part the Red Sea. Then streams of water gushed out from the rock.

"Strike the rock, and water will come out of it, so that the people may drink."

Exodus 17:6

A golden calf

84

God's people did many wrong things as they travelled through the desert from Egypt to the land of Canaan.

One of the worst things they did happened while they were waiting for Moses to come down from Mount Sinai where he was receiving the Ten Commandments.

He [Aaron] took the gold from them, formed it in a mould, and cast an image of a calf.

Exodus 32:4

"GIVE ME YOUR GOLD"

"Go on, Aaron," urged the people, "make us gods to lead us. As for Moses, who knows what's happened to him?"

"Right," replied Aaron, "give me all the gold you can find. Get all the gold earrings you can lay your hands on — from your wives, your sons and your daughters."

Before he had time to think about his wrong actions, Aaron had melted down all the gold and made a beautiful, golden idol, in the shape of a calf.

"Here you are, people of Israel," said Aaron, as the people bowed down in front of the golden calf. "This is the god who brought you out of Egypt!" lied Aaron.

ENTER MOSES

When Moses came down from the top of the mountain, he saw the golden calf. The people were dancing around it.

Then every eye turned towards Moses. He was furious.

He broke the two tablets of stone he was carrying with the Ten Commandments written on both sides.

He snatched hold of the golden calf and melted it down in the fire. He ground all the gold into powder, threw the powder into water, and made the people drink that water.

Spy out the land

86

"HAVE A LOOK AT CANAAN"

God told Moses, "Send one leader from each tribe into the land of Canaan to explore it."

"See if the land is good for fruit or grazing sheep," Moses instructed them.

"Take note of the people who live there," added Moses.

THE NEGATIVE REPORT

After forty days the spies came back with a huge cluster of grapes as well as pomegranates and figs.

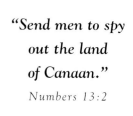

*"Send men to spy
out the land
of Canaan."*

Numbers 13:2

They also brought some pomegranates and figs.

Numbers 13:23

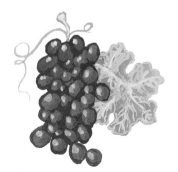

All the spies agreed that the land was lush and perfect for growing fruit.

But nearly all the spies said, "Don't even think about attacking this land!

"The people are very tall and we felt like grasshoppers beside them.

"The towns are so well fortified with their high walls that we wouldn't stand a chance if we tried to capture them."

THE POSITIVE REPORT

Only Joshua and Caleb gave a positive report about the land. They said, "We can take the land for ourselves. We should advance and capture it. We can do it!"

End of an era

88

HELLO JOSHUA

Moses was old and knew that his days were numbered. In front of all of the people he said, "God has told me that I will not be going with you into the Promised Land. But don't be afraid. God will go with you."

Then Moses told Joshua to take over from him as leader of God's people.

Then Moses summoned Joshua . . . in the sight of all Israel.

Deuteronomy 31:7

89

GOODBYE MOSES

Moses climbed to the top of Mount Nebo and looked at all the land God had promised Abraham that God would give to the people. Then Moses, who had been such a close friend of God, died. Moses was buried in the land of Moab, but nobody knows his burial place. The Israelites wept for Moses for 30 days.

Then Moses went up from the plains of Moab to Mount Nebo.

Deuteronomy 34:1

*Then she let them down
by a rope through the
window, for her house
was on the outer side of
the city wall.*

Joshua 2:15

Spies sent to Jericho

JOSHUA TAKES OVER

Moses had died. Joshua had been appointed to take his place.

God said to Joshua, "Be strong and brave. Lead these people to inherit the land that I promised to their ancestors. And remember, I will be with you always, wherever you go."

HELPFUL RAHAB

Joshua wanted to capture the city of Jericho. He wisely sent out two spies to see its precise strength.

The two spies stayed with a woman from Jericho, named Rahab. But someone told the king of Jericho, "Some of those Israelites have entered our city."

"Quick," said Rahab, "the soldiers are looking for you. Go up to the roof. Lie down on the floor." Then Rahab hid them under stalks of flax.

When the soldiers hammered on Rahab's door she said, "Yes, I did see some men, but they left before the city gate was closed for the night."

SECRET SIGNAL

Rahab let the spies down the city wall with a red rope from her window. The spies told Rahab, "Tie this red rope to your window and everyone with you will be kept safe when we attack Jericho."

The battle for Jericho

A STRANGE ENCOUNTER

As Joshua came close to Jericho he was confronted by a man who had a menacing sword in his hand.

"Friend or foe?" stammered Joshua.

"I," the man replied with great dignity, "am the commander of God's army."

No, this wasn't a ghost! Joshua knew he was face-to-face with a messenger from God.

Joshua seemed hardly surprised when he was told, "Take off your sandals. You are standing on holy ground."

Once when Joshua was near Jericho, he looked up and saw a man standing before him with a drawn sword in his hand.

Joshua 5:13

STRANGE TACTICS

Joshua was given a set of very odd-sounding orders by God:

"March round the city of Jericho with your army, once a day, for six days.

"March with priests carrying the holy Ark.

"March with seven priests carrying trumpets made from rams' horns."

Joshua chapter 5 verse 13 to chapter 6 verse 27,

and chapter 8

BLOW THE TRUMPET

"On the seventh day tell the priests to give one long blast on their trumpets," continued God. "Make sure everyone gives a huge cheer! Then the wall will fall down. And the people will go straight into the city."

And that's exactly what happened.

RAHAB IS NOT FORGOTTEN

Rahab remembered to tie the red rope to her window and her family was kept safe.

THE CITY OF AI

Joshua went on to capture the city of Ai by using a cunning ambush, but that's another story.

The troops in ambush rose quickly out of their place and rushed forward.

Joshua 8:19

Jericho

The Old Testament city of Jericho (slightly to the north of the New Testament city) was the oldest walled city in the world. Walls and round stone houses have been excavated dating back to 8,000 BCE.

Desert and mountains lie to the south and west, but at Jericho underground springs created a green oasis. In the Bible, Jericho is nicknamed, "The City of Palms".

Archaeologists have so far found no traces of the massive stone walls of Joshua's Jericho but at the sites of other towns conquered by the Israelites they have found evidence of destruction by fire dating back to the time of Joshua.

Joshua is tricked

94

DIPLOMACY NOT WAR

Not everyone in Canaan resisted Joshua and the Israelites. One group of people, the Gibeonites, decided on diplomacy rather than war.

THE CLEVER PLAN

They knew they could never defeat Joshua, so they decided to trick him into having pity on them.

They searched high and low for anything that was old, musty, torn, worn, cracked, or mended. "I've found those moth-eaten sandals I should have thrown out years ago," cried one of the people of Gibeon.

They put frayed sacks on their donkeys, they wore smelly old clothes, and they put falling apart sandals on their feet.

"LOOK AT OUR BREAD"

"Here's some really stale, mouldy bread," a delighted Gibeonite exclaimed.

When they met Joshua they said, "Look how poor we are. See how mouldy our bread is. We've come such a long way. Will you, please, make a peace pact with us?"

"That won't do," the Israelites replied, "we can't make peace with you if you live near us."

The Gibeonites had an answer for everything. "Oh," a quick-thinking Gibeonite replied, "don't worry yourself about that. We'll be your servants."

The Israelites checked out their story by trying some of their bread. They spat it out of their mouths in disgust as soon as they tasted just how mouldy it was.

A PROMISE OF PEACE

So Joshua promised not to attack the Gibeonites.

Only later did he learn that they lived very close to where he was. He had been completely taken in. He also remembered what he had forgotten. He'd not asked God what to do.

The Gibeonites carried water and cut wood for the Israelites, and were left unharmed.

The inhabitants of Gibeon . . . took . . . worn-out clothes; and all their provisions were dry and mouldy.

Joshua 9:3,5

Joshua chapter 21 verses 1 to 4, chapter 23 and chapter 24

Goodbye Joshua

96

SETTLING DOWN

Under Joshua's dynamic leadership, the people of Israel settled down in the land of Canaan.

The different tribes were given different parts of the land to live in.

The Levites had to sort out where they were going to live. They went and asked Eleazar the priest. They were given towns to live in and pastures to support them, just as God had promised.

FAREWELL SPEECH

God had given the people a safe country to live in under Joshua's wise leadership.

Now Joshua was very old. He knew that he would soon die.

Joshua collected everyone together and told them: "You must throw away the false gods that you worshipped. Love God with all your heart. Keep on obeying God's laws and you will prosper."

"Yes," agreed the people, "we will serve our God."

He [Joshua] took a large stone, and set it up there under the oak in the sanctuary of the LORD.

Joshua 24:26

Chapter 6: From the Bible books of Exodus, Leviticus, Numbers, and Deuteronomy

Learning God's way

INTRODUCTION

The Bible books of Exodus, Leviticus, Numbers and Deuteronomy tell how Moses led God's people through the desert. As they travelled, God gave them laws. Some laws explained how to worship and how to build a holy meeting tent to carry through the desert. Special objects in the tent reminded people about God.

Some laws helped the people to get organized into groups, called the twelve tribes of Israel. The Ten Commandments were an important set of laws to help people relate to God and to each other.

Many laws taught the people kindness, respect, justice and generosity. For example, they were to look after people who didn't have anyone to help them. There were laws about taking care of the land and laws about what foods to eat.

The laws were a gift from God. They helped the people to live well, close to one another and close to God.

The twelve tribes

The twelve tribes of Israel made up God's people, the Israelites. Each tribe was named after one of the twelve sons of Jacob.

They lived in their tribes or clans in the desert.

They pitched their tents in a square formation with God's tent of meeting in their centre.

Three tribes were on the east side, three on the south side, three on the west side and three on the north side.

Exodus chapter 26 and chapter 27 verses 9 to 19

The holy meeting tent

99

*"You shall make the
tabernacle with ten curtains
of fine twisted linen, and
blue, purple, and crimson
yarns; you shall make them
with cherubim skilfully
worked into them."*

Exodus 26:1

Inside God's tent

THE HOLY MEETING TENT

God gave Moses many very detailed instructions about constructing a special tent. Moses said, "I call it the meeting tent. It is where God meets with his people." The tent was a holy meeting place. Only the priests could go inside.

Inside this meeting tent were three carefully made things.

"They shall make an ark
of acacia wood."

Exodus 25:10

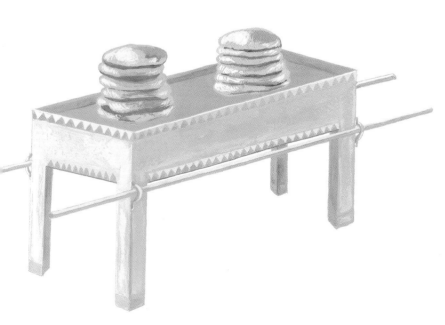

THE ARK

This was also known as the covenant box. A man called Bezalel made it of acacia wood. He overlaid the wooden box with gold.

On its lid Bezalel hammered gold into the shape of two creatures with wings. They faced each other and their wings spread across the top of the box.

The two flat stones with the Ten Commandments on them were placed inside the ark.

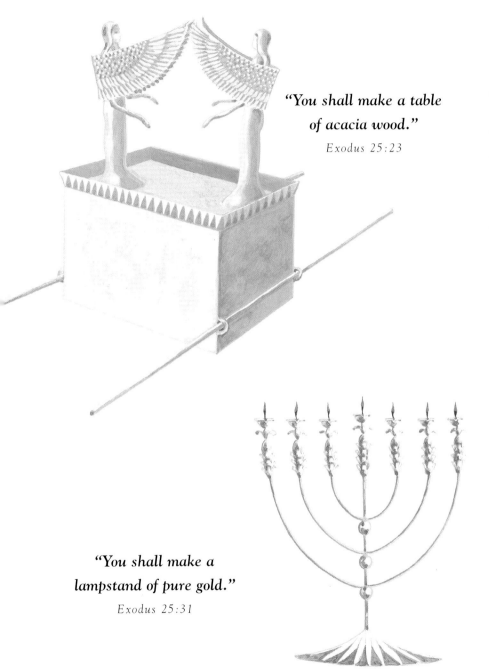

"You shall make a table of acacia wood."

Exodus 25:23

THE TABLE

A table, also made out of acacia wood and covered with pure gold, also stood inside God's holy meeting tent. On this table golden plates had bread on them that was offered to God.

THE LAMPSTAND

God also told Moses, "Make a lampstand out of pure gold." It had to have three branches on each side, making seven in all. These became seven small oil lamps.

"You shall make a lampstand of pure gold."

Exodus 25:31

Sacrifices for God

102

THE COURTYARD

Outside God's tent, but enclosed in a fence of curtains was a large courtyard where the people could go. In this courtyard God told Moses to have two things made.

THE ALTAR

God told Moses to have a square-shaped altar made. Each corner of the altar had to stick out like a horn. It was made out of acacia wood, covered in bronze. This was used for burning the sacrifices — the sheep and goats.

Special pots were made to remove the ashes. Shovels and bowls were made for sprinkling the blood. Then there were large meat forks, as well as pans for carrying the burning wood. All these had to be made of bronze.

"You shall make the altar of acacia wood . . . and you shall overlay it with bronze."

Exodus 27:1-2

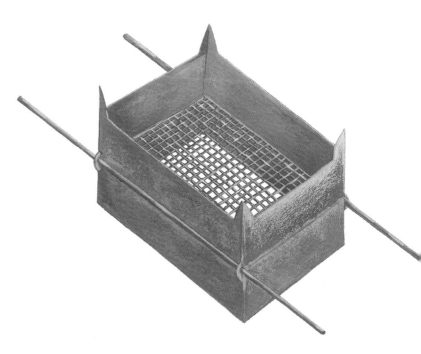

*"You shall make all of its
utensils of bronze."*

Exodus 27:3

THE BRONZE BOWL

Before the priests entered the tent of meeting or
sacrificed any of the animals God ordered that they
should wash their hands and feet. Water for this was
put in a large bronze bowl which had its own bronze
stand.

Poles and rings

All the objects inside and
outside God's meeting tent
were portable. They could
be easily carried around by
the Israelites as they pitched
camp in different places in
the desert.

The ark of the covenant,
the table and the bronze
altar were all fitted with
four rings through which
two carrying poles fitted. In
this way everything could be
easily carried.

Special clothes

104

PRIESTS

The people who looked after the sacrifices around God's special tent were called priests. They had special, holy work to do for God, so God ordered that they should wear special clothes.

God told Moses, "Tell your brother Aaron and his children to serve me as priests. Make holy clothes for Aaron that will give him beauty and honour."

Aaron was the first chief priest and was called the high priest.

"Make the outer robe to be worn under the holy robe, using only blue cloth."

Exodus 28:31 (ICB)

"Make the woven inner robe of fine linen. Make the turban of fine linen, also."

Exodus 28:39 (ICB)

The Day of Atonement

The first goat

Once a year, on the Day of Atonement, the high priest sprinkled blood from a killed goat on the ark of the covenant in God's meeting tent.

This was God's way of teaching the people how innocent blood was shed instead of the people who had sinned against God.

The second goat

The high priest then took another goat, placed his hands on its head, and confessed the sins of God's people. This goat was known as the scapegoat. This goat was set free in the desert and, symbolically, carried away the people's sins.

The names of the sons of Israel were carved on these 12 jewels as a person carves a seal.

Exodus 39:14 (ICB)

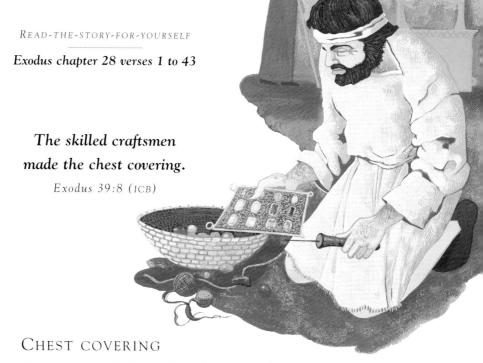

The skilled craftsmen made the chest covering.

Exodus 39:8 (ICB)

CHEST COVERING

God also told Moses that Aaron had to wear a special chest covering.

It had four rows of beautiful gems on it.

The first row of jewels had a ruby, a topaz and a yellow quartz.

The second row had a turquoise, a sapphire and an emerald.

The third row had a jacinth, an agate and an amethyst.

On each of the twelve jewels was engraved the name of one of the twelve tribes of Israel.

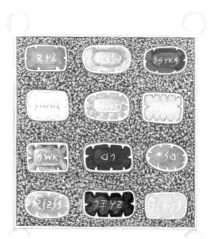

Everybody is involved

106

Each of the twelve tribes of Israel brought gifts for God's meeting tent. Each tribe brought the same number and same kinds of gifts.

THE GIFTS

Each tribe brought one silver plate, one silver sprinkling bowl, one gold dish, one young bull, one ram and one lamb for a burnt offering, one goat for a sin offering, two oxen, five rams, five goats, and five lambs as a fellowship offering.

Sacrifices

The burnt offering
The animal or bird was killed and completely burned.
    This symbolized the wish to be rid of sin.

The sin offering
The animal or bird was sacrificed. This symbolized the sins of the Israelites being "paid off".

The fellowship offering
An animal was sacrificed. This symbolized the people's wish to give thanks.

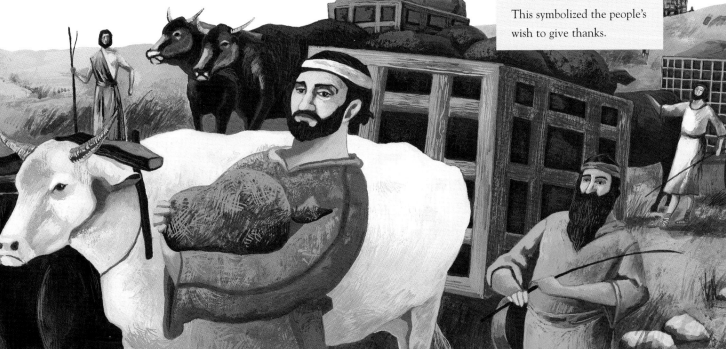

107

Festivals

Trumpets were to be blown
to announce festivals and
celebrations.

These festivals, which
were times of great
celebration, reminded God's
people of God's great care for
them.

The Feast of Trumpets
This celebrated the New Year.

New Moon Festival
This was held at the start of
each month.

The Feast of Shelters
This reminded the people of
their time in the desert. They
built shelters of branches and
lived in them for a week.

*The Passover and Feast of
Unleavened Bread*
This celebrated the time
when God rescued the people
from Egypt, when God passed
over them (that is, spared
them).

The Feast of Weeks or Harvest
The Israelites offered God
the first crops from their
harvest, thanking God for all
the crops.

MOVING GOD'S TENT

When the Israelites moved on to a different place they
took God's special tent with them.

It was all very organized. Everybody knew what
they had to do.

The Levites were in charge of carrying the ark.

The Gershon family, under the direction of High
Priest Aaron, had to carry all the coverings of the
meeting tent. They were also responsible for folding
up and transporting the curtains of the courtyard that
surrounded the holy tent.

> *"They shall carry . . .
> the tent of meeting with
> its covering."*
>
> *Numbers 4:25*

The Ten Commandments

108

Three months to the day after the Israelites left Egypt they arrived at the Desert of Sinai.

God called Moses to the top of Mount Sinai and there gave the Ten Commandments.

COMMANDMENTS ONE TO FOUR

1 "Do not have any other gods
   except for me."

2 "Do not make any idols."

3 "Do not misuse God's name."

4 "Keep the Sabbath as a holy day."

*Israel camped there [in
the wilderness of Sinai]
in front of the mountain.*

Exodus 19:2

COMMANDMENTS FIVE TO TEN

5 "Respect your parents."

6 "You must not murder anyone."

7 "You must not commit adultery."

8 "You must not steal."

9 "You must not tell lies about your neighbour in court."

10 "You must not want things that don't belong to you."

In the desert God continued to care for and look after the people. God gave them laws to live by, laws to help them.

God even made sure that slaves were protected from being mistreated by their masters. If a master knocked out a slave's tooth, the master had to free that slave.

"He [God] . . . will bless your cows with calves and your sheep with lambs."

Deuteronomy 7:13 (ICB)

Freedom and justice for all

110

BE KIND TO EACH OTHER

God told Moses to tell the people to care for each other.

"Don't cheat one another.

"Don't be unkind to blind or deaf people.

"Look after people who don't have anyone to care for them.

"Always remember how you felt as slaves in Egypt, and treat others better."

CARE FOR THE LAND

God also wanted people to take care of the land. "You may live on it, but it belongs to me," God explained.

Seven was a special number to remember. Every seventh year was to be a year of rest for the land — just as every seventh day of the week was a day of rest for the people. God said that in the seventh year people shouldn't plant seeds, plough, or cut down vines; but they could eat whatever grew naturally.

You shall love the LORD your God with all your heart, and with all your soul, and with all your might.

Deuteronomy 6:5

You shall love your neighbour as yourself.

Leviticus 19:18

Leviticus chapter 25, and Deuteronomy chapter 15 verses 1 to 18

You shall have the trumpet sounded throughout all your land. And you shall hallow the fiftieth year and you shall proclaim liberty throughout the land to all its inhabitants.

Leviticus 25:9-10

A HOLY YEAR

Every fiftieth year was a very holy year, a year of jubilee. A trumpet blast would announce that everyone was to be free from debt and slavery.

Sometimes people became so poor that they sold their land to pay debts. "On the fiftieth year, all the land goes back to its original owners," said God. Sometimes people had to sell their house to buy food. In the jubilee year, the houses had to be given back. Sometimes people became so poor they sold themselves, and worked like slaves, "Don't make people slaves," said God. "On the fiftieth year all the debts must be forgiven. Set everyone free." This rule wasn't just for the Israelites, it was for everyone, even foreigners.

IMPORTANT LAWS

The laws helped the women and men understand that they were people who followed God. Some laws became central to the life of the Jewish people. Two laws were quoted by Jesus as the greatest commandments (see captions on page 110).

Laws to live by

In the desert God gave Moses all kinds of laws. As well as religious laws there were laws about how to help foreigners and strangers and not to take revenge.

LAWS ABOUT WHAT TO EAT

God knew that not all animals and plants were fit for humans to eat.

God said that the people were not to eat pigs. God knew what food would keep the people healthy and strong so God told them not to eat things like rats and lizards.

Some of the food laws were also religious laws. They helped the people to remember, in everyday ways like eating, that they were different and that they followed God and not the gods of other peoples around them.

"You shall not do as they do in the land of Canaan, to which I am bringing you. You shall not follow their statutes . . . You shall keep my statutes."

Leviticus 18:3-4

Chapter 7: From the Bible books of Numbers, Judges and Samuel

The judges and Samson

INTRODUCTION

As they marched towards Canaan, the Israelites spread fear among their enemies. A talking donkey had to teach a foreign prophet a lesson.

The judges of Israel were leaders, commanders-in-chief during times of war, and judges who settled arguments the Israelites had among themselves, during times of peace.

We are also introduced to Samuel who, when he was still a boy, heard God calling him in the night.

In these pages we meet the famous woman judge, Deborah, Jael and her tent peg and hammer, Gideon and his army, which God told him to reduce from 32,000 to 300, and Samson and his bulging muscles.

Balaam's talking donkey

114

THE PEOPLE OF MOAB ARE SCARED

On their way to the land of Canaan the Israelites had to pass close to the land of Moab, where Balak was the king. The people of Moab were terrified.

"Look, there are so many of them," said the people of Moab, shaking with fear. "This mob will take everything we have. They'd be like an ox eating up all the grass."

The donkey saw the angel of the LORD standing in the road . . . so the donkey turned off the road and went into the field.

Numbers 22:23

THE KING SENDS FOR BALAAM

"Go and get that prophet, Balaam," bellowed King Balak.

"He's a prophet," said Balak. "It's his job to curse people. We'll pay him lots of money and get him to put a curse on these people who've come up from Egypt."

BALAAM HITS OUT AT HIS DONKEY

God didn't want Balaam to go and told him that, if he did go, he must say only what God told him.

Balaam set out riding his faithful donkey. Suddenly, the donkey saw an angel standing in the path. The angel had a drawn sword. If they moved forward, they would be killed on the spot.

So the donkey left the path and went into a field. Balaam lashed out at the donkey, hitting with a stick. "Get back on to the road," he yelled.

Later, the path narrowed as it went between two vineyards with a wall on each side. The donkey saw the angel again and bumped into one of the walls, hurting Balaam's foot. Balaam hit out at the poor donkey again.

Balaam listens to the donkey

116

THE TALKING DONKEY

The third time the angel appeared, the donkey just sat down. Balaam beat the donkey again. "Why have you hit me three times?" the donkey asked.

Balaam forgot that donkeys don't speak and replied, "You've made a fool of me. If only I had a sword to hand, I'd use that on you!"

The donkey carried on the conversation, "Have I ever acted like this before?"

"No," admitted Balaam, thoughtfully.

When the donkey saw the angel of the LORD, it scraped against the wall, and scraped Balaam's foot.

Numbers 22:25

BALAAM SEES THE ANGEL

When God saw that Balaam was willing to listen to a donkey and to admit that he may not be aware of everything that's going on, God let Balaam see the angel with the sword. Balaam fell to the ground and bowed low.

"I did wrong. I did not know you were standing in the road," explained Balaam.

BALAAM DOES NOT CURSE THE ISRAELITES

By the time Balaam finished his journey he knew what God wanted him to say. His message to King Balak was, "I am telling you only what God tells me to say. God is with these people. They are as strong as a lioness. Anyone who blesses these people will be blessed. Anyone who curses these people will be cursed."

As a result of this, King Balak did not attack the Israelites.

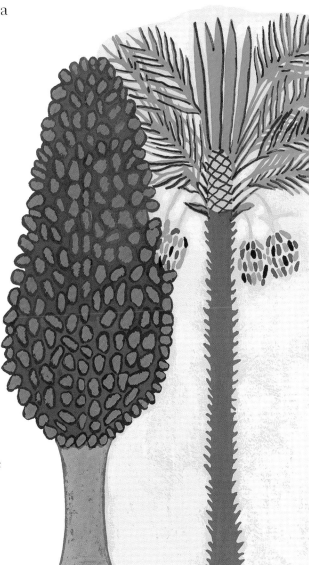

After Joshua

118

DISOBEYING GOD

It was so sad. Despite everything Joshua had said — about obeying God and keeping God's laws — the Israelites started to worship the gods of the people who lived around them.

GOD'S ACTION

God was angry with the people for disobeying. So God allowed the people to be robbed and defeated by their enemies.

THE PEOPLE ASK FOR GOD'S HELP

Then the Israelites turned back to God in their hearts and cried out, "Oh, God, we're in such a mess. Save us from our enemies."

JUDGES TO THE RESCUE

Then God chose people who were called "judges" to lead the Israelites. So long as God's people obeyed God they defeated their enemies.

DEBORAH, THE JUDGE

Deborah, a prophet, was also a judge of the Israelites. Often as Deborah sat under her favourite palm tree, people brought their disagreements to her. If someone was accused of a crime, Deborah judged the case and decided what the wrongdoer must do to make amends.

STOP SISERA'S ARMY

One day, Deborah sent for Barak. "God says you're to gather 10,000 men to fight Sisera," she said. Barak was scared. Sisera, a Canaanite general, was a powerful enemy. He had over 900 iron chariots. For twenty years, the people had suffered under his cruel hand.

"God has promised us help," Deborah assured him. "I'll go," Barak said nervously, "but only if you go with me."

Deborah agreed, but she had a warning for Barak. "You're not going to be the hero. Sisera will be defeated, but by a woman."

She used to sit under the palm of Deborah . . . and the Israelites came up to her for judgment.

Judges 4:5

A brave woman

Israel's judges

The book of Judges
The sixth book of the Bible
is called the book of Judges.
It records the lives of the
people who led the Israelites
after Joshua died, but before
they had any kings to rule
over them.

Judges
These judges were not
exactly like the judges in
our law courts today. It is
true that they acted like
modern judges and settled
disputes between people
who came to them, but they
were also rulers and military
leaders.

The Bible mentions 13
of these rulers, the most
famous one being Samson.

Sisera was running away from Barak. He came to the
tent of a strong woman named Jael. "Come in here
and rest, my Lord," invited Jael. Sisera drank
refreshing milk from Jael's leather bag and curled up in
a blanket.

Jael drove a tent peg right through Sisera's head as
he slept. He died without feeling a thing.

Then Deborah and Barak sang a hymn together.

"I myself will sing to the Lord.

I will make music to the Lord, the God of Israel . . .

Let all the people who love you be powerful like
the rising sun."

And there was peace throughout the country for a
very long time.

*But Jael, the wife of
Heber, took a tent peg
and a hammer.*

Judges 4:21 (ICB)

Strange maths

GIDEON'S ARMY

When Gideon led God's people, the Midianites were their number one enemy.

But Gideon thought that he could defeat them. After all he now had 32,000 soldiers. Gideon couldn't believe his ears: "You've got too many men," God told him. "If you defeat the Midianites with that kind of strength, the Israelites will never stop boasting about their power."

FROM 32,000 TO 10,000

So Gideon reluctantly told his troops, "Anyone who'd really rather be at home than fighting this war can leave." So 22,000 soldiers ran home. But that still left a fighting force that was 10,000-strong.

FROM 10,000 TO 300

Next Gideon took his men to drink from a stream. Nearly all of them, 9,700 to be exact, knelt down and lapped the water up. But 300 men scooped up some water in their hands and drank the water from their cupped hands.

"Right," God informed Gideon, "I'm going to deliver you from the Midianites with just those 300 men."

Judges chapter 6 verse 33 to chapter 7 verse 25

The LORD said to Gideon,
"The troops with you are
too many . . . Israel
would only take the credit
away from me, saying,
'My own hand has
delivered me.'"

Judges 7:2

NIGHT ATTACK

In the middle of the night Gideon's faithful 300 men
surprised the mighty Midianite army with their
unexpected attack. The Midianites all panicked and
ran off.

God calls a child

124

HANNAH PRAYS FOR A BABY

Hannah knelt in the temple. Tears ran down her cheeks as she prayed, "God, if only you will give me a baby, then I promise that I will let the child serve in your temple."

Eli, the priest, thought Hannah was drunk until she told him how much she longed for a baby.

"Go in peace," said Eli, "God has heard you."

Hannah did have her baby, a wonderful little boy. She called him Samuel.

When Samuel was old enough, he went to work as a helper in the temple, just as Hannah had promised.

GOD CALLS SAMUEL BY NAME

One night, when Samuel was still just a child, he was lying on his mat in the dark temple. He heard a voice calling, "Samuel, Samuel."

Samuel thought it was the old priest, Eli. "Here I am," he called. Eli woke up. "Go back to bed, I didn't call you," said Eli sleepily.

The LORD called, "Samuel! Samuel!" And he said, "Here I am!"
1 Samuel 3:4

1 Samuel chapter 1 verse 1 to chapter 4 verse 1

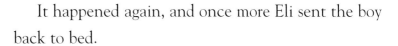

125

It happened again, and once more Eli sent the boy back to bed.

The third time, Eli figured it out. "It's God calling you," he said, and he told Samuel what to do.

The next time God called, Samuel was ready. "Speak God, for your servant is listening," he said.

SAMUEL, THE TRUSTED PROPHET

Samuel grew up very close to God and became a wise prophet. All of God's people trusted Samuel. They knew when he spoke, that it was God's word they were hearing.

The times of the judges had been difficult. The people longed for a king — someone who would end the fighting in the land, someone who would bring them all together as one great nation.

They begged the prophet Samuel to ask God to give them a king. Samuel didn't think this was such a great idea. He talked it over with God many times. Finally, God helped Samuel to choose a king for the Israelites.

Samson, the strongest

A STRANGE MARRIAGE

In Samson's time, Israelites and Philistines were
enemies. Samson should not have married Timnah, a
Philistine. But Samson wouldn't listen to anyone. At
his marriage feast he teased the Philistines. "If you
answer my riddle, I'll give you 30
sets of clothes. If you don't, you
owe me clothes."

THE RIDDLE

"Out of the eater comes something to eat, out of
the strong comes something sweet. What is it?"
Samson was thinking of a lion carcass he'd seen.
Inside it, bees had made sweet honey.

Samson said to them,
"Let me now put a riddle
to you."

Judges 14:12

Judges chapter 13, 14 and 15

The Philistines didn't have a clue. But they forced
Timnah to tell them.

THE ANSWER

"What could be sweeter than honey? What could be
stronger than a lion?" said the Philistines smugly.
Samson boiled with rage, but he gave them the
clothes.

SAMSON, THE STRONG

Samson is very strong, but not very wise. He doesn't
listen to his people and he drifts away from God. As
biblical storytellers show, his pride gets in the way
once too often, and the Philistines defeat him.

> *On the fourth day, they
> said to Samson's wife,
> "Coax your husband to
> explain the riddle to us."*
>
> *Judges 14:15*

Samson defeated

128

Samson fell for Delilah, a beautiful but bad woman. The Philistines longed to know the secret of Samson's strength. They said to Delilah, "If you tell us why Samson is so strong, we'll give you a whole sack of silver."

"Samson," purred Delilah, "if you loved me, you'd tell me the secret of your strength."

"Bind me with seven new bowstrings and I'll be weak as a baby," lied Samson. Delilah tried that but Samson broke them easily.

"Samson, my love, if you really, really loved me, you'd tell me what makes you strong," Delilah persisted.

"Cut off my hair," said Samson. This was Samson's big mistake. His long hair showed that he was supposed to be dedicated to God, but Samson never took that seriously. He never thought anyone could defeat him.

While Samson slept, Delilah called a man who cut his hair. He became weak and the Philistines captured him.

The lords of the Philistines came to her [Delilah] and said to her, "Coax him, and find out what makes his strength so great, and how we may overpower him."

Judges 16:5

Chapter 8: From the Bible books of Ruth, 1 Samuel, 2 Samuel, 1 Kings and 2 Kings

David takes on Goliath

INTRODUCTION

This chapter opens with the tale of Ruth and her great loyalty. The story starts with Ruth living in a foreign country with her mother-in-law, who does not have a penny to her name. But the story ends with Ruth marrying one of the richest men in Bethlehem. History also remembers Ruth for being King David's grandmother.

In another exciting tale, David unexpectedly defeats the giant, Goliath.

The sad decline of Saul, Israel's first king, is eclipsed by the wonderful reign of Israel's greatest king — David.

The queen of Sheba's spectacular visit to Solomon comes next.

A glimpse of the prophetic career of Elijah follows.

And finally, there is the story of an unnamed young slave girl who helps a powerful army general to find a cure for his leprosy.

The story of Ruth

FAMINE STRIKES BETHLEHEM

There was a terrible famine in Israel. Naomi, her husband, and her two sons left their home in Bethlehem to find food. They travelled to the land of Moab, even though Moab and Israel were enemies.

In Moab, there lived a beautiful Moabite woman named Ruth. One of Naomi's sons married Ruth. But tragedy struck again. Naomi's husband and two sons died. Naomi had no one to support her.

The famine is over, so I will go back home," Naomi decided.

FAITHFUL RUTH

Ruth insisted on staying with Naomi, while Naomi's other daughter-in-law went back to her own home. Ruth said to Naomi, "Don't ask me to leave you. Don't beg me not to follow you. Every place you go, I will go. Every place you live, I will live. Your people will be my people. Your God will be my God."

RUTH MEETS BOAZ

Naomi and Ruth had no money. So Ruth went out to a field to collect the grains of barley that had fallen to the ground during the harvest.

Boaz, the rich man who owned the field, strolled up at lunchtime. He'd heard how Ruth helped Naomi. He gave Ruth some lunch. Ruth was very surprised.

At the mealtime, Boaz
said to her, "Come here
and eat some of this
bread . . ." She ate until
she was satisfied, and she
had some left over.

Ruth 2:14

Boaz marries Ruth

Now this was the custom . . . to confirm a transaction,
one party took off a sandal and gave it to the other.

Ruth 4:7

Ruth chapters 3 to 4

Selling Naomi's land

Naomi's land
Naomi had to sell the land that had belonged to her dead husband. Women weren't allowed to own land in those days. The law said the closest relative must be given the first chance to buy the land, so that it stayed in the family.

The town gate
The place to do business was the town gate. Boaz went there with ten town leaders to help settle the matter.

Boaz makes a deal
Boaz was related to Naomi, but he wasn't the closest relative. And the closest relative wanted Naomi's land. "That means you'll have to take care of Ruth and Naomi," said Boaz. "No way!" said the relative, "I don't want the extra burden. You can have the land." He took off his sandal — a sign that he meant it.

Then Naomi took the child and laid him in her bosom, and became his nurse.

Ruth 4:16

Boaz was related to Naomi and Ruth.

He wanted to help them so he decided to buy the land that Naomi's husband had once owned. Then he married Ruth.

GRANDMOTHER NAOMI

Naomi became the happiest grandmother in the world when a baby boy was born to Boaz and Ruth.

The baby's name was Obed. Obed had a famous grandson, the most famous king of Israel, King David.

134

David takes on the giant

A sling

David's sling was made from a small leather pouch into which a 3½ cm stone could fit snugly. This pouch was tied to two cords of rope, each 60 cm long. As the sling was whirled around, the stone stayed in the pouch. But as soon as one of the strings was released the stone would fly out with great force.

Soldiers and slings

Some soldiers were trained to be specialists in using slings. Such soldiers always hit their targets. "700 of these trained soldiers were left-handed. Each of these left-handed soldiers could sling a stone at a hare and not miss!"

David and his sling

Just because Goliath was a giant it looked as if David must be defeated. But David used his sling to protect his sheep by frightening off bears. Goliath did not stand a chance!

GOLIATH ROARS

"What a lot of cowards you are," bellowed Goliath, the giant Philistine. "Who's going to fight me today?" he roared, as he waved his gigantic spear.

"Send one of your men to fight me," challenged the Philistine champion. "If he wins, the Philistines will be servants to you Israelites. But if I win . . . hah, hah, hah!!" Goliath's words trailed off into a roar of menacing laughter.

When the Philistine drew nearer to meet David, David ran quickly towards the battle line . . . David took out a stone, slung it, and . . .

1 Samuel 17:48,49

DAVID TRUSTS IN GOD

David stepped forward.

"I'll fight you, Goliath," the teenage shepherd said.

"You may well have a sword, a large spear and a small spear to help you. But I have the Lord of heaven's armies on my side. I trust in God," said David bravely.

"When I've defeated you," continued David, "everyone will know that God does not need swords and spears to save people."

LET THE CONTEST BEGIN

David took out his trusted sling. He put in one of the five smooth stones he had just picked up from the river bed.

Whirl, whiz, splat.

The stone found its target — Goliath's forehead.

David killed the giant.

Against all the odds, Israel had beaten the Philistines.

. . . struck the Philistine on his forehead; the stone sank into his forehead and he fell face down on the ground.

1 Samuel 17:49

Israel's first king

Saul sought to pin David to the wall with the spear; but . . . David fled and escaped that night.

1 Samuel 19:10

ISRAEL ASKS FOR A KING

The people of Israel wanted to be like all the other countries around them. They longed for their own king.

SUCH A PROMISING START

Saul, a man head and shoulders taller than everyone else, became the first king of Israel.

All seemed to be going so well. The prophet Samuel had anointed Saul with oil. The Israelites were winning victories over their enemies.

EATEN UP BY JEALOUSY

Saul often felt depressed. But he was soothed by David playing music on his harp.

But after David defeated Goliath, the people's favourite song rang in Saul's ears:

"Saul has killed thousands of his enemies.

But David has killed tens of thousands."

Saul was green with envy. He tried to kill David by pinning him to the wall with his spear.

Saul chased David all over the country, but David escaped each time.

SUCH A SAD END

Saul was a broken man. He turned away from trusting in God. He broke the law by going to see a medium, that is, someone who talked with spirits of dead people.

The next day the Philistines killed Saul's three sons in battle. When Saul saw that he had lost, he took his own sword, threw himself on it, and died.

So Saul disguised himself and put on other clothes and . . . came to the woman by night.

1 Samuel 28:8

137

David: Israel's greatest king

138

ISRAEL'S SECOND KING

After Saul's death, David became king of Israel.

David's army captured Jerusalem by climbing up the water tunnel and surprising the soldiers.

It happened late one afternoon, when David rose from his couch and was walking about on the roof of the king's house, that he saw from the roof a woman bathing: the woman was very beautiful.

2 Samuel 11:2

David made all the Israelites one great nation. He made Jerusalem the capital. And he brought the holy ark of God into the centre of the city.

GREAT WEAKNESS

David's greatness lay in his great love for God. But King David also had weaknesses.

He spotted the beautiful Bathsheba bathing herself. He wanted her. He was king. So he slept with her. As soon as David heard that Bathsheba

was going to have his baby he arranged for Bathsheba's husband, Uriah, to be killed in battle.

But David did tell God how sorry he was for taking someone else's wife, and for what amounted to murder. David prayed, "God, be merciful to me . . . wipe out all my wrongs" (Psalm 51:1 ICB).

GREAT STRENGTH

David was great, not just because he won many battles but also because he was kind.

David asked Ziba, a servant from Saul's family, "Is anyone left in Saul's family?"

"One of Saul's grandsons is still alive," replied Ziba. "His name is Mephibosheth. He can barely walk."

Mephibosheth hobbled into King David's presence. He was afraid, because Saul had been David's enemy.

"Mephibosheth," declared David, "you and your family will always eat at my table."

Mephibosheth could hardly believe his ears.

David said to him, "Do not be afraid, for I will show you kindness for the sake of your father Jonathan."

2 Samuel 9:7

1 Kings chapter 10 verses 1 to 13

King Solomon

A ROYAL VISITOR

After King David died, his son Solomon became king. Solomon built a magnificent temple for God in Jerusalem.

One day Solomon had a special visitor, the Queen of Sheba. And she did not arrive empty-handed. The queen brought Solomon gifts: four tons of gold, spices, and jewels. Later, someone wrote, "No one since that time has brought more spices into Israel than the Queen of Sheba gave King Solomon."

WISDOM

The Queen of Sheba heard that Solomon was very wise, so she tested him with hard questions. Solomon answered brilliantly.

"God has given you this wisdom so that you can be a good and fair king," declared the queen. Then the Queen of Sheba left for home with her endless line of camels.

When the queen of Sheba heard of the fame of Solomon (fame due to the name of the LORD), she came to test him with hard questions.

1 Kings 10:1

The dynamic duo

142

Then he [Elisha] set out
and followed Elijah, and
became his servant.

1 Kings 19:21

ELIJAH AND ELISHA

Many of the later kings of Israel disobeyed God. But the worst one of all was King Ahab. With his equally wicked wife, Jezebel, Ahab worshipped the so-called god of the weather, Baal, instead of God.

At this time God sent two prophets to speak up for God. Elijah was the senior prophet and Elisha was his assistant. Elisha took over when Elijah died.

A DROUGHT

Elijah told King Ahab that God would bring a drought. "There will be no rain or dew for the next few years," predicted Elijah.

King Ahab was furious. All the

1 Kings, chapters 17, 18 and 19

The jar of meal was not emptied, neither did the jug of oil fail, according to the word of the LORD.

1 Kings 17:16

prophets of Baal did their best to produce rain. But no rain came.

Later, just after Elijah said to the king, "A heavy rain is coming," it rained and rained and rained.

ELIJAH AND THE WIDOW

During the drought, God told Elijah to go to the town of Zarephath. There, Elijah saw a poor widow gathering sticks. Hungry and thirsty from his long journey, he asked her for bread and water.

The woman sighed. "All I have is a handful of flour and a spoonful of oil. I was just going to bake one last loaf of bread. My son and I will have nothing to eat after that, so we'll certainly die."

Elijah looked her in the eyes. "Don't be afraid," he said. "Bake me a small loaf with what you have, and God will make sure you are never hungry."

The brave woman trusted God. She used her last bit of flour and oil to make a meal for Elijah.

A miracle happened! The woman's jars of oil and flour were never empty again.

General Naaman's illness

144

General Naaman commanded the army of the king of Aram. He'd won victory after victory. But one thing made him desperately sad. He suffered from a dreaded skin disease. People said: "Don't go near Naaman. He's a leper!"

A YOUNG GIRL

Naaman's wife had a young slave girl. She had been taken as a captive from Israel in one of the raids by the Arameans. She said to Naaman's wife, "I know a man from my country who could heal General Naaman."

So the general visited the prophet Elisha, and was told, "Go and wash in the River Jordan."

When Namaan did this he was cured. His skin became like that of a young child.

[Naaman] came and stood before him [Elisha] and said, "Now I know that there is no God in all the earth except in Israel."

2 Kings 5:15

Chapter 9: From the Bible books of Esther, Job, and Psalms

Praising through problems

INTRODUCTION

This chapter starts with the book of Esther, which tells how a beautiful queen saved the Jews throughout the Persian Empire from a holocaust. It then focuses on the sad plight of Job wallowing in a heap of ashes, beside himself with wounded pride and a body full of agonizing sores.

The book of Psalms follows. In the psalms all the feelings that we have ever had are there somewhere. The psalms are different kinds of prayers and songs. In the psalms there are prayers asking God for things and prayers thanking God for being so wonderful.

But there are also the kinds of prayers that we may not often dare pray. There are prayers telling God how fed up, or sad, or angry we feel.

Esther saves the Jews

ESTHER BECOMES QUEEN

Long after Jerusalem was destroyed, the Jews who had been taken as captives were living in the cities of the Persian Empire. Esther was a beautiful young Jew. Her parents had died, so Esther was cared for by her uncle Mordecai.

One day, the king sent his servants to find the most beautiful woman in the empire to be his queen. Esther was chosen. Before she left for the palace, Mordecai made her promise not to tell anyone that she was Jewish.

A PLOT TO KILL THE JEWS

Haman was one of the king's top officials. Everyone bowed down to him—everyone, that is, except Mordecai. This made Haman furious. He planned a way to kill Mordecai.

Haman went to the king. "The Jews aren't obeying your laws," he lied. He persuaded the king to sign a letter which would let Haman kill all the Jews in the empire.

Uncle Mordecai told Esther of the plot. "Pray for me," said Esther. "I'll do what I can."

ESTHER SPEAKS UP

Anyone who approached the king without being called could be killed. In spite of the danger, Esther went to the king and invited him to come to dinner with her.

Meanwhile, Haman built a gallows on which to hang Mordecai.

ESTHER SAVES HER PEOPLE

The king came to eat at Esther's special dinner. He offered to give Esther anything she wanted. Esther told the king about Haman's plan to kill Mordecai and all the other Jews.

"I want you to save my people," she told the king. "That is my request."

The king was so shocked that he ordered Haman to be hanged on the very gallows he had made for Mordecai. The king sent out an order that the Jews should be spared.

The Jews held a great party to celebrate. "Esther has saved us!" they cheered.

Then Esther said in reply to Mordecai, ". . . I will go to the king, though it is against the law; and if I perish, I perish."

Esther 4:15-16

Job's suffering

148

"My skin hardens, then
breaks out again."

Job 7:5

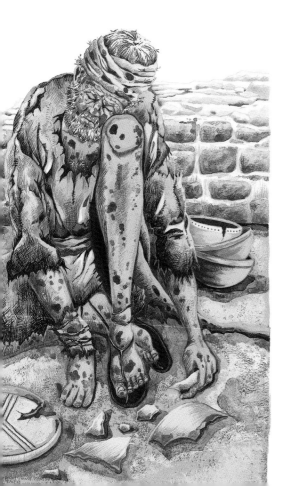

SATAN'S CHALLENGE

One day Satan, one of the heavenly beings, said to God, "If you took away all the blessings you've given to your servant Job, I bet he would curse you."

"We'll see about that," replied God. "Everything Job has is in your power."

SATAN ATTACKS

Satan was quick to act.

He killed off Job's 500 pairs of oxen,

he killed off Job's 500 donkeys,

he killed off Job's 7,000 sheep,

he killed off Job's 3,000 camels.

Then he killed off Job's sons and daughters.

JOB'S SORES

Then Satan attacked Job. Job had painful sores all over him, from the top of his head to the tips of his toes. He tried to reduce his pain by scraping himself with broken pieces of pottery. He was in a terrible state.

JOB'S WIFE GIVES ADVICE

"Go on, Job," egged on Job's wife. "Be done with it. Curse God and die."

"You shouldn't say such a thing," countered Job, "we accept good things from God's hands. Shouldn't we also accept trouble from God?"

ADVISORS GALORE

Job was not short of other advice. One, two, three, four friends came and told Job why he was in such a mess. But none of them helped Job.

Job noted that wisdom was more valuable than rubies, even though some people spend all their energy digging up precious stones from mines.

"Miners put an end to darkness, and search out to the farthest bound the ore in gloom and deep darkness."

Job 28:3

Elihu's advice

"For to the snow God says,
'Fall on the earth.'"

Job 37:6

At last, Job's first three friends stopped speaking.

At least Job's fourth friend, Elihu, had something positive to say:

"Look at God's greatness," suggested Elihu. "Look at the storm clouds, look at the rain, look at the snow. Think about the sun and its golden light. God is so wonderful. God is so powerful. God is never unkind."

GOD'S ADVICE

Job begged God to explain why he was in so much pain. He heard God ask these questions:

"Who made the world? Who made the earth? Who made the sea?"

Job bowed his head.

"Will anyone argue with the all-powerful God and correct me?" continued God. "Look at this behemoth, this huge creature! Look at its bulging muscles. Look at how powerfully it can swim."

151

Reading the book of Job

The 42 chapters of the book of Job can be a little confusing when they are read for the first time.

Chapters 1 to 2
These chapters tell how Satan attacks Job.

Three comforters
Job discusses his plight with three people who have been called "comforters" but who often give Job advice that is far from helpful.

Comforter No 1 is Eliphaz (Job chapters 4-7; 15-17; 22-24).

Comforter No 2 is Bildad (Job chapters 8-10; 18-19; 25).

Comforter No 3 is Zophar (Job chapters 11-14; 20).

A fourth friend
Elihu adds in his more helpful suggestions in chapters 32-37.

God's reply
Job sees God's greatness in chapters 38-42.

"Look at Behemoth, which I made just as I made you."

Job 40:15

JOB WORSHIPS GOD

Job bowed his head even lower.

"Yes, God, I agree," said Job humbly. "Everything you do is wonderful."

God made Job better again, gave him a new family, and even more oxen, sheep and donkeys.

Psalm 23

The LORD is my shepherd.
Psalm 23:1

This is the most famous of the 150 psalms and is probably the best-known chapter in the Bible. One way of reading the psalm is to read it from the point of view of a sheep. Imagine that you are a sheep as you read it.

THE SHEEP'S PSALM

"The LORD is my shepherd.

I have everything I need.

He gives me rest in green pastures.

He leads me to calm water.

He gives me new strength.

For the good of his name,

he leads me on paths that are right.

Even if I walk

through the dark valley of death,

I will not be afraid

because you are with me.

Your rod and your staff comfort me."

Psalm 23:1-4 ICB

Looking at the details

There are many details in this psalm that should not be missed.

"Green pasture" verse 2
This stands for everything that makes you strong and healthy.

"God leads me" verse 2
Even today in the Middle East the shepherd does not drive sheep from behind, but leads them from the front, and they follow.

"Calm water" verse 2
Calm waters were a safe place for the sheep to drink.

"Your rod and your staff comfort me" verse 4
Sheep were often in danger of being attacked by bears and lions. A shepherd's rod, like a 1¼ m club, protected the sheep.

The shepherd's 2 m staff guided the sheep and kept them from straying into danger.

Thanking God for. . .

154

GOD'S HELP

In Psalm 121 we can imagine the writer looking out over the fields towards the distant hills. They look so powerful and strong.

Then the psalmist remembers where human strength comes from. It is a gift from God.

"The LORD protects you as the shade protects you from the sun. The LORD will guard you from all dangers . . . the LORD will guard you as you come and go, both now and for ever." Psalm 121:5, 7, 8 ICB

I lift up my eyes to the hills — from where will my help come? My help comes from the LORD, who made heaven and earth.

Psalm 121:1-2

Psalms 121 and 67

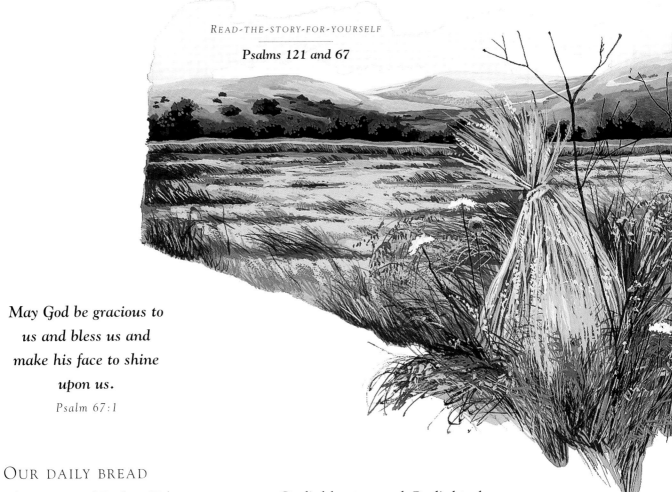

May God be gracious to
us and bless us and
make his face to shine
upon us.

Psalm 67:1

OUR DAILY BREAD

The writer of Psalm 67 longs to receive God's blessing and God's kindness.

Then the writer recalls how much God is always blessing us, rescuing us from danger, and how much the whole world should give thanks to God.

"God, have mercy on us and bless us.

Show your kindness to us.

Then the world will learn your ways.

All nations will learn that you can save.

God, the people should praise you." Psalm 67:1-3 ICB

Prayers for every kind of mood

156

WHEN I AM SAD

Some of the psalms were written by King David.

When David prayed, he told God about his bad moods as well as his good moods.

Psalm 102 records the prayer of a person who is suffering. The psalmist does not try to hide sad feelings from God, but tells God how awful everything seems.

God, I feel like that owl I saw the other day in the desert, says Psalm 102. "I am like an owl living among the ruins. I lie awake. I am like a lonely bird on a housetop . . . My tears fall into my drink."

"But," adds Psalm 102, "Lord, you rule for ever." Psalm 102:6-7, 9, 12 ICB

I am like an owl of the wilderness, like a little owl of the waste places.

Psalm 102:6

Psalms 102 and 139

GOD KNOWS EVERYTHING

157

In Psalm 139 David is cheered up when he remembers that God knows everything about him. He reminds himself that he was made by God.

". . . You know all about me . . . You made my whole being.

You formed me in my mother's body. I praise you because you made me in an amazing and wonderful way. What you have done is wonderful. I know this very well." Psalm 139:1, 13-14 ICB

For it was you who formed my inward parts; you knit me together in my mother's womb.

Psalm 139:13

*The king of Egypt
sent for Joseph
and freed him.*
Psalm 105:20 ICB

Learning from the psalms

A HISTORY LESSON

Each of the 150 psalms has something to teach us.

Psalm 105 is like a history lesson. It goes over the history of God's people, the Israelites, saying how much God always showed his love for them.

JOSEPH

Do you remember Joseph?

"God ordered a time of hunger in the land.

And he destroyed all the food.

Then he sent a man ahead of them.

It was Joseph, who was sold as a slave.

They put chains around his feet and an iron ring around his neck.

Then the time he had spoken of came.

The Lord's words proved that Joseph was right.

The king of Egypt sent for Joseph and freed him.

The ruler of the people set him free."

Psalm 105:16-20 ICB

FINDING THE WAY

Psalm 119 is the longest psalm.

Its message is that God guides all who go through life following his word.

Your word is a lamp to my feet and a light to my path.

Psalm 119:105

159

Songs of praise

160

MUSICAL INSTRUMENTS

The psalms are full of verses that tell us that we should praise God — that we should sing to God — that we should play instruments to make music for God.

"Praise him with stringed instruments and flutes.

Praise him with loud cymbals.

Praise him with crashing cymbals.

Let everything that breathes praise the Lord.

Praise the Lord!" Psalm 150:4-6 ICB

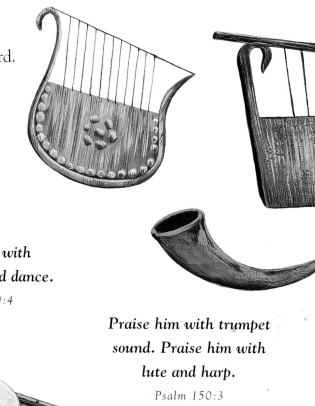

Praise him with tambourine and dance.

Psalm 150:4

Praise him with trumpet sound. Praise him with lute and harp.

Psalm 150:3

Chapter 10: From the Bible books of Proverbs, Ecclesiastes,
and the Song of Solomon

Stunning words of wisdom

INTRODUCTION

This chapter introduces us to a great biblical character, a woman named
Wisdom, who is a central figure in the book of Proverbs. Proverbs is
crammed full of advice on how to be wise. It was written especially for young
people.

The book of Ecclesiastes follows. The big question this book asks is,
"How can you be happy in life?" It mentions all kinds of things which do not
bring deep happiness.

The next book, the Song of Solomon, is a book for people in love. It's a
love song written by a king.

Proverbs galore

162

WISDOM FOR YOUNG PEOPLE

If you like quotations, or wise sayings, or clever sounding one-liners, then the book of Proverbs is for you.

There is only one book in the Bible that was especially written for young people. It is the book of Proverbs.

SOLOMON SPEAKS UP

The opening verses of the book of Proverbs introduce the book.

"These are the wise words of Solomon, son of David, king of Israel."

Let the wise also hear and gain in learning.

Proverbs 1:3

Proverbs chapter 1 verses 1 to 7, and chapter 8 verses 1 to 14

"These words teach wisdom and self-control.

They give understanding . . .

They will teach you what is honest and fair and right.

They give the ability to think to those with little knowledge.

They give knowledge and good sense to the young . . .

Knowledge begins with respect for the Lord." Proverbs 1:1-4, 7 ICB

THE MOST VALUABLE THING IN THE WORLD

Wisdom is more valuable than the most precious jewels, more valuable than pearls, even more valuable than rubies.

For wisdom is better than jewels, and all that you may desire cannot compare with her.

Proverbs 8:11

All kinds of wisdom

Wisdom cries out in the street; in the squares she raises her voice.

Proverbs 1:20

WISDOM IS CALLING

The book of Proverbs tells of a wise woman who was God's helper in creation. Her name is Wisdom.

Wisdom calls out from the busy street corner. "Pay attention. I have something important to tell you. Trust in God with all your heart," she says.

Wisdom sighs sadly. No one is listening. They prefer not to know. "What will you do when you get into difficulty?" Wisdom asks. "If you don't have me to help, you are going to be in big trouble."

A child who sleeps in harvest brings shame.

Proverbs 10:5

165

Collected sayings

1 Kings 4:32 records that King Solomon told 3,000 proverbs, and it is very likely that Solomon was the source of many or most of the proverbs in the book of Proverbs (see 1:1). Other proverbs came from a man called Agur, from a King Lemuel and from unnamed wise men (22:17).

Some of Solomon's sayings were copied down by "King Hezekiah's men" (25:1). Nobody is sure when all the proverbs were finally collected together. But the purpose is clear: to teach God's people to live wisely. And "wise" people are not the brainy types, but those who know how God wants them to behave — and do it.

LAZINESS NEVER PAYS

The book of Proverbs has many verses telling its readers not to be lazy.

"A lazy person will end up poor" (Proverbs 10:4 ICB).

Lazy people are always making excuses.

"The lazy person stays in bed and turns over and over" (Proverbs 26:14 ICB).

Nuggets of wisdom

166

RESPECT YOUR PARENTS

Mums and dads are meant to teach everything that is good to their children. That's why the book of Proverbs says that children should follow the advice of their parents.

"A wise child loves discipline, but a scoffer does not listen to rebuke" (Proverbs 13:1 NRSV).

Hear, my child, your father's instruction, and do not reject your mother's teaching.

Proverbs 1:8

Proverbs from Proverbs

A number of the sayings in the book of Proverbs can be found in many books of quotations because they are so striking.

Anger
"A soft answer turns away wrath" (Proverbs 22:1).

A happy heart
"A happy heart is like good medicine" (Proverbs 17:22 ICB).

Starting right
"Train children in the right way, and when old, they will not stray" (Proverbs 22:6).

Tomorrow
"Don't brag about what will happen tomorrow. You don't really know what will happen then" (Proverbs 27:1 ICB).

A SUPER-MUM AND SUPER-WIFE

In the last chapter of the book of Proverbs, chapter 31, there is a description of a mother who is creative, hard-working, and generous. She makes clothes for her family and is up at the crack of dawn to prepare the meals for each day.

In contrast to the idle person of Proverbs 26:15, this super-mum, "Looks well to the ways of her household, and does not eat the bread of idleness. Her children rise up and call her happy; her husband too, and he praises her" (Proverbs 31:27, 28 NRSV).

The lazy person buries a hand in the dish, and is too tired to bring it back to the mouth.

Proverbs 26:15

Spot the difference

168

PLENTY OF FOOD
These two pictures may
remind you of those puzzles
which ask you to see how
many differences you can find
between the two pictures.

*Those who till their
land will have plenty
of food . . .*
Proverbs 12:11

No food

169

The first picture is the result of hard work, which produces plenty of food.

The second picture is the result of no work, which produces no food.

The book of Proverbs also says:

"Hard workers will become leaders" (Proverbs 12:24 ICB).

"Evil people want what other evil people have stolen" (Proverbs 11:12 ICB).

> ***. . . but those who follow***
> ***worthless pursuits have***
> ***no sense.***
>
> *Proverbs 12:11*

More helpful advice

Don't be proud

Proverbs hits out against pride. It is not good to think you're better than others.

"It is wise to hate pride and bragging, evil ways and lies" (Proverbs 8:13 ICB).

"Pride leads only to shame. It is wise not to be proud" (Proverbs 11:2 ICB).

"Pride leads to arguments" (Proverbs 13:10 ICB).

When pride comes, then comes disgrace.

Proverbs 11:2

Proverbs chapter 8 verse 13, chapter 11 verses 2 and 13, chapter 16 verse 28, and chapter 26 verse 20

171

The words of a whisperer are like delicious morsels.

Proverbs 18:8

DON'T GOSSIP

The book of Proverbs says that even though people like saying nasty things about others, to do so is wrong.

"A person who gossips can't keep secrets" (Proverbs 11:13 ICB).

"A person who gossips ruins friendships" (Proverbs 16:28 ICB).

"Without wood, a fire will go out. And without gossip, quarrelling will stop" (Proverbs 26:20 ICB).

Self-control

TOO MUCH WINE

While some people think that there's nothing wrong with getting drunk, the book of Proverbs has a different view.

"Some people drink too much wine.

They try out all the different kinds of drinks.

So they have trouble. They are sad.

They fight. They complain.

They have unnecessary bruises.

They have bloodshot eyes.

Don't stare at the wine's pretty red colour.

It may sparkle in the cup.

It may go down your throat smoothly.

Do not look at wine . . .
when it sparkles in
the cup.

Proverbs 23:31

Proverbs chapter 23

Like a city breached,
without walls, is one
who lacks self-control.

Proverbs 25:28

But later it bites like a snake.
Like a snake, it poisons you"
(Proverbs 23:29-32 ICB).

TEMPER, TEMPER

We all lose our temper sometimes. But the book of
Proverbs says how good it is to keep
ourselves under control.

"Patience is better than strength.
Controlling your temper is
better than capturing a city"
(Proverbs 16:32 ICB).

What makes you happy?

WISDOM

Money and food do not bring happiness that lasts, says
the book of Ecclesiastes. Only wisdom does that.

"Wisdom is better than money" (Ecclesiastes 7:12 ICB).

"Wisdom gives a person strength" (Ecclesiastes 7:19 ICB).

The lover of money
will not be satisfied
with money.

Ecclesiastes 5:10

Ecclesiastes chapter 7 verses 1 to 29, and chapter 3 verses 1 to 7

A time, a place for everything

175

"There is a right time for everything.

Everything on earth has its special season.

There is a time to be born

and a time to die.

There is a time to plant

and a time to pull up plants.

There is a time to kill

and a time to heal.

There is a time to destroy

and a time to build.

There is a time to cry

and a time to laugh.

There is a time to be sad

and a time to dance . . .

There is a time to be silent

and a time to speak."

Ecclesiastes 3:1-4, 7 ICB

Go, eat your bread with enjoyment, and drink your wine with a merry heart.

Ecclesiastes 9:7

Song of Solomon chapter 8 verses 6 to 7 and verses 13 to 14

In love

176

A LOVE SONG

In the original Hebrew, the opening words are: "Solomon's Song of Songs". This can mean that the Song is about, or for, or by King Solomon.

MANY PICTURES

The song uses many images: the lover is like a gazelle, a wild dove, or a beautiful garden. Nothing can drown love.

"Love is as strong as death.

Desire is as strong as the grave.

Love bursts into flames.

It burns like a very hot fire.

Even much water cannot put out the flame of love.

Floods cannot drown love."

Song of Solomon 8:6-7 ICB

Be like a gazelle or a young stag upon the mountains of spices!

Song of Solomon 8:14

Chapter 11: From the Bible book of Isaiah

Isaiah's message of hope

INTRODUCTION

The contrasting messages of Israel's greatest prophet, Isaiah, take up this whole chapter.

Isaiah's dire warnings about God's judgment seem hard.

But Isaiah had to deal with major problems: How could he shake such a proud people out of their complacency? How could he stop them relying on and worshipping their man-made idols? How could he stop them cheating and mistreating the poor?

Yet Isaiah also has many messages of hope.

He pictures a future time when the wolf and lamb will live together peacefully. He talks of a new city made of jewels and, best of all, a time of peace when God's people will be able to enjoy the fruit of their own gardens.

"Look out, Jerusalem!"

178

TWO KINGDOMS

The country David and Solomon had ruled had split into two. Isaiah warned the northern kingdom, called Israel, that they would be invaded by the Assyrians.

Isaiah, God's prophet, warned the southern kingdom, Judah, that they also would be destroyed.

PROUD PEOPLE

But the people had no time to listen.

"Come on," the rich people of Jerusalem said to each other, "let's strut around the town. And don't forget your jewellery, dazzling bracelets, and fancy robes."

"You cheat the poor to get rich," accused Isaiah. "You crush God's people, grinding their faces into the dirt."

What do you mean by crushing my people, by grinding the face of the poor? says the Lord God of hosts.

Isaiah 3:15

My vineyard

179

THE SONG ABOUT THE VINEYARD

"Listen to my song about the vineyard," said Isaiah. "My friend who had a vineyard on a hill, did everything possible to get the best grapes.

"My friend planted the best grapevines and built a watchtower to protect the vineyard.

"But it only produced bad grapes.

"Now I'm going to destroy my vineyard."

Isaiah explained the song. "You people are the vineyard — God planted you. God expected justice, kindness and goodness, but all he hears is crying."

God expected justice, but saw bloodshed; righteousness, but heard a cry!

Isaiah 5:7

Parables

Jesus wasn't the only person who told parables. Isaiah the prophet told a parable about vines.

Vineyards
Vineyards stood for God's people, the Israelites.

Hills
Vines were planted on hills so they had good drainage and so they caught the sun.

Watchtower
While the upper part of the tower was a lookout post to spy on enemies, the lower part was lived in during the harvest.

Winepress
This was a basin-shaped hole cut out of a rock. Workers would stomp on the grapes until the juice spilled out and collected in the hole.

Remember Israel

THEY WERE WARNED

"God punished the people of Israel," reminded Isaiah, "because they cut themselves off from God through their evil."

"Evil is like a small fire," the prophet continued, "which starts off as a small bonfire, just burning weeds and thorns. Then it spreads and larger bushes catch alight. After that it turns into a forest fire as the trees catch fire. The whole forest goes up in a column of smoke. All the people will be burned up like that."

Isaiah chapters 10 to 11

The cow and the bear shall graze, their young shall lie down together.

Isaiah 11:7

The light of Israel will become a fire, and his Holy One a flame.

Isaiah 10:17

HOPE FOR ISRAEL

Although Israel and Judah were both conquered by foreign powers, the prophet Isaiah looked forward to a time when God would bring peace.

"Then wolves will live in peace with lambs.
And leopards will lie down to rest with goats.
Calves, lions and young bulls will eat together.
And a little child will lead them.
Cows and bears will eat together in peace.
Their young will lie down together.
Lions will eat hay as oxen do." Isaiah 11:6-7 ICB

Other nations beware

182

EGYPT

The prophet Isaiah did not restrict his warnings to Israel
and Judah, where God's people lived. He also warned
that God would punish other countries because of
their evil. Even the super-power, Egypt, would
suffer.

"The sea will become dry.

The water will disappear from the
Nile River.

The canals will stink.

The streams of Egypt will
decrease and dry up.

All the water plants will rot.

All the plants along the banks
of the Nile will die."

Isaiah 19:5-7 ICB

*The waters of the Nile
will be dried up.*

Isaiah 19:5

Isaiah chapter 19, and chapter 21 verses 1 to 10

Babylon

Another country which seemed to be all-powerful would also be defeated. The Babylonians captured Jerusalem, but, said Isaiah, "God is even stronger than the mighty Babylonians."

"A lookout," predicted Isaiah, "will see men riding on chariots and horses, donkeys and camels. One of these cries out, 'Babylon is fallen. It has fallen!'"

Babylon

Babylon the mighty
Babylon was Judah's enemy. The Babylonians surrounded and defeated Jerusalem and took the Jews off to Babylon into exile. Nobody could resist their armies.

Prophecy against Babylon
Yet Isaiah the prophet predicted the time when Babylon would itself be crushed.

God would break "the staff of the wicked, the sceptre of rulers, that struck down the peoples . . . that ruled the nations in anger with unrelenting persecution" (Isaiah 14:5-6).

Babylon did fall
Babylon was indeed defeated on October 16, 539 BCE, when the Persian king, Cyrus, entered Babylon.

"Don't be so proud!"

THE POTTER

"Stop telling God what God should be doing," was
Isaiah's message.

"Look at a potter who is in charge of a lump of clay.
The potter makes whatever the potter likes with it.

"You Israelites are the clay. God is the potter. But
you are telling the potter what to do. The pot is telling
its maker, 'You don't know anything.'"

DON'T TRUST ARMIES

Judah's leaders wanted to make a deal with Egypt.
"Their chariots and horses may look powerful,"
warned Isaiah, "but they won't save you."

Isaiah longed for people to stop trusting

*"Shall the thing made
say of its maker, 'He did
not make me'?"*

Isaiah 29:16

Isaiah chapter 29 verses 15 to 16, and chapter 31 verse 1 to chapter 32 verse 14

"The palace will be forsaken, the populous city deserted."

Isaiah 32:14

armies and start trusting God. "Then you will
have good leaders," said Isaiah. "Wicked rulers leave people
hungry but good leaders bring justice.

"If you don't listen, the palaces will be empty. Strong cities and towers will end up
in ruins. Wild donkeys and sheep will graze there."

"I have called you . . . to
open the eyes that are
blind, to bring out the
prisoners from the
dungeon."

Isaiah 42:6-7

Isaiah chapter 42 verses 1 to 9, and chapter 44 verses 9 to 20

Future hope

Isaiah told the people of Jerusalem that one day
God would send a very special messenger.

"God will do amazing things," enthused Isaiah.

"God will be a light for all the people.

God will help the blind to see.

God will set the prisoners free from prison.

God will lead those who live in darkness into light."

THE CAUSE OF THE PROBLEM

Isaiah said that God's special messenger would not
allow idols to be worshipped in God's place.

"Can't you see," stormed Isaiah, "how useless idols are?"

"Think about it. Think how idols are made," reasoned Isaiah.

"You cut down a cedar, cypress or oak tree. Half the wood you
chop up for winter fires. Some of the wood is used for your oven
to bake bread. Then you take some of the wood, make an idol
and worship it. How crazy can you get?!"

"Can't you see how silly this is? You take wood from a tree,
use some of it to heat your home and bake your bread, then you
fall down and worship the rest of it."

**Then he makes a god
and worships it.**

Isaiah 44:15

Hope in days of disaster

PROTECTION

"You trusted armies and idols and bad leaders more than God. You hurt the poor. And now terrible things are happening. But God has not forgotten you." This was Isaiah's message in a nutshell.

God still loved the people. God was going to send them a deliverer. This person would be like a razor-sharp arrowhead and would have great power to defeat any enemy. This deliverer would have great strength because the strength came from God.

A NEW CITY

Isaiah gave God's people many messages of hope. Although he said Jerusalem would be destroyed, he painted a picture of a new city that God would give to the people.

"You poor city. Storms have hurt you, and you have not been comforted.

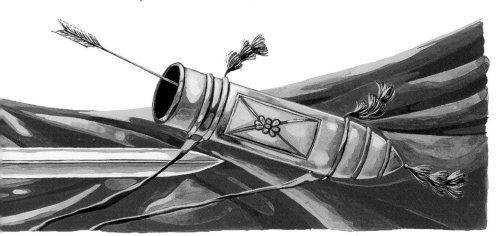

God made my mouth like a sharp sword, in the shadow of God's hand God hid me.

Isaiah 49:2

But I will rebuild you using turquoise stones.

I will build your foundations with sapphires.

I will use rubies to build your walls.

I will use shining jewels for the gates.

I will build all your outer walls from precious jewels." Isaiah 54:11-12 ICB

I will make your pinnacles of rubies, your gates of jewels.

Isaiah 54:12

No peace for the wicked

But the wicked are like the tossing sea that cannot keep still.

Isaiah 57:20

190

"God plans to bless you," said Isaiah excitedly. "He will give peace to everyone, far and near, and he will heal you."

"But," thundered Isaiah, "this is not the case for evil people. For evil people are like the restless, angry sea. Its waves toss up dirt and mud. 'There is no peace for evil people,' says my God."

Isaiah chapter 57 verses 14 to 21, and chapter 60 verses 1 to 9

*Lift up your eyes and
look around; they all
gather together.*

Isaiah 60:4

191

FROM DARKNESS
TO LIGHT

"Jerusalem is a doomed city,"
explained the faithful prophet,
"but one day it will be a blessed city."

> "Jerusalem, get up and shine.
> Your light has come.
> The glory of the Lord shines on you.
> Darkness now covers the earth.
> Deep darkness covers her people.
> But the Lord shines on you,
> and people see his glory around you . . .
> Look around you.
> People are gathering and coming to you.
> They are your sons coming from far away.
> And your daughters are coming with them.
> When you see them, you will shine with happiness." Isaiah 60:1-5 ICB

Peace will dawn

192

God's people longed for peace. "Will we ever stop living in fear of our enemies?" they wondered.

Isaiah ended the book with this message of hope.

"In that city the person who builds a house will live there.

The person who plants vineyards will get to eat grapes.

No more will one person build a house and someone else live there.

One person will not plant a garden and someone else eat its fruit.

My chosen people will live there and enjoy the things they make." Isaiah 65:21-22 ICB

They shall plant vineyards and eat their fruit.

Isaiah 65:21

Chapter 12: From the Bible books of Jeremiah and Lamentations

Jeremiah's prophecies

INTRODUCTION

This chapter is about Jeremiah, a prophet in Jerusalem who started preaching when he was a teenager.

The time came when God's people were under siege in the great city of Jerusalem. Food and water were running out. Outside the walls, the Babylonian army was preparing battering rams to crash into Jerusalem.

God gave Jeremiah a message for the rulers in Jerusalem: "Don't resist the king of Babylon; his army will destroy Jerusalem and take you as captives to Babylon."

Sharing this message made Jeremiah sound like a traitor. The rulers did everything they could to silence Jeremiah. His scroll was burned. He was put in prison. He was thrown into a well. But Jeremiah's prophecies came true.

Then God's people remembered what else Jeremiah had prophesied — that God would return them to their homeland.

God calls Jeremiah

194

TOUCHED BY GOD

God spoke to Jeremiah out of the blue one day, "Jeremiah, I have chosen you to be my prophet."

"You must be joking," protested Jeremiah. "I'm only a teenager."

"Don't say you aren't old enough," God replied, "I knew you when you were a lot younger. When you were

"Now I have put my words in your mouth."

Jeremiah 1:9

Jeremiah chapter 1 verses 4 to 10, and chapter 7 verses 1 to 15

*"If you do not oppress
the alien, the orphan
and the widow . . . then
I will dwell with you."*

Jeremiah 7:6-7

still curled up inside your mother's womb, I decided that you would speak for me."

God touched Jeremiah on the lips. "See, I've put my words inside you," God said gently. "Don't be afraid. I'll be right there with you."

JEREMIAH'S MESSAGE

"Jeremiah," said God, "go and stand at the gate of the temple. Here is the message you are to deliver."

Jeremiah obeyed. "Listen, people of Jerusalem, this is God's message.

"If you want to keep living in Jerusalem, change your lives. Stop lying and stealing. Stop cheating and hurting one another. Stop mistreating people who have no one to protect them. Take care of widows and foreigners and orphans.

"Don't listen to the people who say, 'We have God's temple. We have God's temple.' Saying that isn't going to save them. They must come back to God and do what's right."

God warns Jerusalem

"Are the birds of prey all around her?"

Jeremiah 12:9

It wasn't as if God's people had not been warned. They had turned away from God. They now worshipped idols. Jeremiah said that God would bring them back to their senses by punishing them.

God said, "You will become like a bird that birds of prey attack. You will be attacked by wild animals. Shepherds will ruin your vineyards and trample on the plants in the fields."

Jeremiah chapters 12 and 14

MORE TRAGEDY

The people of Jerusalem suffered a terrible drought. There was no rain. The wells ran dry. They were desperate for water.

Servants came back from the wells with empty jars. The ground was dry and cracked and the farmers were despairing. God's people turned back to God and said, "God is our only hope."

"God is so sad about what is happening," said Jeremiah. "God is crying like a parent who has lost a child."

"They come to the cisterns, they find no water, they return with their vessels empty."

Jeremiah 14:3

The broken jar

198

Jeremiah was fed up. He'd never wanted to be a prophet in the first place. Now he was given a most unpopular message. And nobody took any notice of him.

God said to Jeremiah, "Buy a clay jar, and then while the people with you are watching, break the jar. Then say this:

'The Lord of heaven's armies says: I will break this nation and this city just as someone breaks a clay jar. It cannot be put back together again.

'. . . I said I would bring disaster to Jerusalem and the villages around it. I will make it happen soon! This is because the people are very stubborn. They do not listen at all to what I say.'" Jeremiah 19:10-11, 15 ICB

"Then you shall break the jug in the sight of those who go with you."

Jeremiah 19:10

The LORD showed me two baskets of figs.

Jeremiah 24:1

Exiled

Jeremiah's prophecies about God's people being taken off from Jerusalem by their conquerors proved true.

605 BCE
Some people were carted off by King Nebuchadnezzar in 605 BCE See Daniel 1:1-2.

597 BCE
Among the 10,000 prisoners exiled in 597 BCE were the leaders, the craftspeople and metal workers and all the wealthy people of Jerusalem. Only the poorest people in the land were left. See 2 Kings 24:14.

586 BCE
In 586 BCE, the skilled craftspeople who had escaped exile in 597 BCE, along with some of the very poor people, were rounded up by King Nebuzaradan and herded off to Babylonia.

199

Two baskets of figs

Jeremiah was given a vision by God. "Perhaps this will wake up the people of Jerusalem," thought Jeremiah to himself.

"I can see two baskets of figs," declared Jeremiah. "One basket is full of lovely, ripe, juicy figs," Jeremiah continued, "while the other basket is full of rotten figs which nobody can eat."

"The good figs," explained God, "are the good people. Although I will send the people of Judah out of their country to Babylon, I will bring them back to the land of Judah. I will not destroy them, but will plant them so they can grow. They will want to know me."

"But the bad figs," concluded God, "are King Zedekiah and his advisors who still live in Jerusalem."

Jeremiah's unpopular message

200

Do not listen to them;
serve the king of Babylon
and live.

Jeremiah 27:17

Everyone in Jerusalem hated the world's leading
superpower, the Babylonians. "So," the people of
Jerusalem reasoned, "it's Jeremiah's job to tell us
that God will deliver us from those dreadful
Babylonians. Why doesn't Jeremiah tell us that
God will work some miracle for us?"

Jeremiah put a yoke of straps and poles on the back of his neck. Then he said to
Zedekiah, king of Judah, who lived in Jerusalem:

"You must surrender to the king of Babylon and serve him. If you serve him and
his people, you will live. Don't listen to people who say differently: the false prophets,
people who use magic to tell the future, those who say they can interpret dreams,
mediums and magicians."

TAMBOURINES

Jeremiah delivered many messages of hope to God's people. In different ways Jeremiah said, "If you trust in God, God will bless you. This will be a time to bang your tambourines, to dance and to be joyful."

"Look, the time is coming," says the Lord,
"when I will make a new agreement.
It will be with the people of Israel
and the people of Judah.
. . . I will put my teachings in their minds.
And I will write them on their hearts.
I will be their God,
and they will be my people."
. . . I will forgive them for the
wicked things they did."
Jeremiah 31:31, 33, 34 ICB

*Again you shall take
your tambourines and
go forth in the dance of
the merrymakers.*

Jeremiah 31:4

Verses to note

Apart from being Jeremiah's greatest prophecy, Jeremiah 31:31-34 is unique in two ways.

Longest quotation
Jeremiah 31:31-34 is the longest passage from the Hebrew Scriptures to be quoted in the New Testament. See Hebrews 8:8-12.

A new covenant
Verse 31 of Jeremiah chapter 31 speaks about a new agreement, or new covenant. The name that is used for the second part of our Bible, the New Testament, is taken from this word "agreement", or "covenant".

Was Jeremiah a traitor?

JEREMIAH'S SCROLL BURNED

God said to Jeremiah, "Take a scroll. Write on it everything that I have told you about Israel, Judah and the other nations."

"Baruch," Jeremiah called to his scribe, "I've got a big writing job for you." Baruch wrote all of Jeremiah's message in ink on a scroll. Jeremiah said, "Now take the scroll and read it to all the people in the temple."

"Your Majesty," said the king's officials, "Jeremiah has written a terrible scroll."

King Jehoiakim ordered one of his officials, Jehudi, to read the scroll.

Jehudi began to read, but after he had read three or four columns, the king cut the columns off the scroll with a penknife and threw them into the fire. Finally the whole scroll was burned.

Immediately, Jeremiah began to write a new scroll.

SPEAKING OUT

Later, when Zedekiah was king of Judah, God told Jeremiah to take a message to the palace.

"What with all these unpatriotic words I'm supposed to say, people will think I'm a traitor," Jeremiah worried.

This was God's message to King Zedekiah:

"I will hand the city of Jerusalem over to the king of Babylon and he will burn it

Jeremiah chapter 36 and chapter 38

down. You will not escape from the army of Babylon.
You will be caught and taken to Babylon as a captive."

King Zedekiah got so angry that he ordered
the palace guard to seize Jeremiah and
keep him under lock and key.

*As Jehudi read three or
four columns, the king
would cut them off with
a penknife and throw
them into the fire in the
brazier.*

Jeremiah 36:23

Ink

Baruch used ink
Baruch said, "I wrote down
all the words with ink on
this scroll" (Jeremiah 36:18
ICB).

This is the only place in
the Hebrew Scriptures
where ink is mentioned.

Making ink
In Jeremiah's day, ink was
made from soot or
lampblack (a black colloidal
substance made mostly of
carbon). This was then
mixed with arabic gum or
oil.

Into the well

THE EGYPTIAN ARMY

The palace guards got so sick of Jeremiah's constant preaching they threw him into an empty well. The view from the bottom of the well was bleak. As Jeremiah shivered with cold and sank into the wet mud, he thought, "Is this where I'm going to be left to die?"

"All I did was to tell King Zedekiah what God told me to say: 'The army of the king of Egypt came to Jerusalem to help you against the Babylonian army. But the Egyptians will return to Egypt. Then the Babylonian army will defeat Jerusalem and burn it.'"

GOOD OLD EBED-MELECH

Jeremiah's friend, Ebed-Melech, risked his own neck. He went to King Zedekiah, and bravely said: "Your majesty, Jeremiah the prophet has been thrown into a well. Soon he will die there. This is wrong."

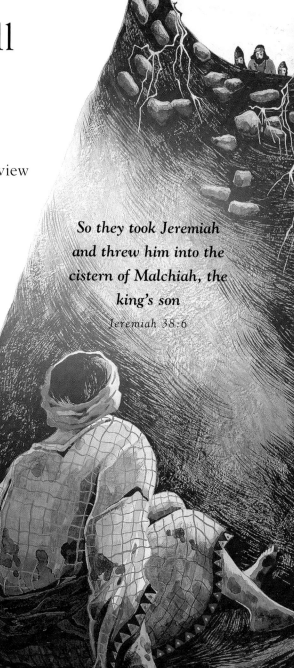

So they took Jeremiah and threw him into the cistern of Malchiah, the king's son

Jeremiah 38:6

Jeremiah chapter 38, and chapter 49 verses 7 to 22

The king ordered Ebed-Melech to mount a rescue operation. With the help of 30 men and a lot of rope, Ebed-Melech hoisted Jeremiah to safety. Jeremiah thankfully breathed the fresh air. But he was still a prisoner of the court guard.

"Although you make your nest as high as the eagle's, from there I will bring you down," says the LORD.

Jeremiah 49:16

A MESSAGE FOR EDOM

Jeremiah was given messages by God for other nations. Many of these nations hated the Israelites and attacked them. They thought that might was right and that they could get away with anything.

Edom was one of those nations. Its big problem was giant-sized pride. Jeremiah told Edom, "You can't escape from God."

"'Edom, you frightened other nations.
Your pride has fooled you.
You live in the hollow places of the cliff.
You live on the high places of the hills.
Even if you build your home as high as an eagle's nest,
I will bring you down from there!' says the Lord."
Jeremiah 49:16 ICB

There is still hope

*One runner runs to
meet another, and one
messenger to meet
another.*

Jeremiah 51:31

Everybody in Jerusalem now knew that they were no
match for the mighty armies of Babylon. But Jeremiah told them that this would not
always be the case.

This is how Jeremiah put it, "This is what the Lord says: 'I will cause a destroying
wind to blow. It will blow against Babylon and the Babylonian people.'"

Jeremiah imagined the impossible: "One messenger follows another. Messenger
follows messenger. They announce to the king of Babylon that his whole city has
been captured." Jeremiah 51:1, 31 ICB

Jeremiah chapters 51 and 52

Jerusalem falls

The Babylonian army surrounded Jerusalem. They waited it out until there was no food left in the city. King Zedekiah and his army fled from Jerusalem and tried to outrun the Babylonian army. But the Babylonian army chased them, and caught up with Zedekiah and his soldiers. Zedekiah was given a terrible punishment. The last thing he ever saw was his sons being killed before him. Then he was blinded. He was taken to Babylon in a bronze chain, like an animal. He was kept in prison there until he died.

With no army left to defend Jerusalem, the Babylonians walked into the city and burned it to the ground. The war was over — Jerusalem had fallen.

The king of Babylon took him [Zedekiah] to Babylon, and put him in prison until the day of his death.

Jeremiah 52:11

207

Crying over Jerusalem

208

All her people groan as they search for bread; they trade their treasures for food.

Lamentations 1:11

The long book of Jeremiah is followed by a short book, called the book of Lamentations. It has five sad songs about Jerusalem.

Lines from the first lament record the plight of Jerusalem. "The enemy reached out and took all her precious things. She even saw foreigners enter her Temple . . . All of Jerusalem's people are groaning. They are looking for bread. They are giving away their precious things for food so they can stay alive." Lamentations 1:10, 11 ICB

Sing a sad song

Jeremiah lived through the terrible events described in these funeral songs and it is thought that he wrote Lamentations. In the sadness, there is light: "The Lord's love never ends . . . The Lord is what I have left. So I have hope" (3:22, 24 ICB). After 70 years the Jews were allowed to go back and rebuild the city.

Every Friday Jews in Jerusalem go to the "Wailing Wall" where they read aloud from Lamentations.

Chapter 13: From the Bible books of Ezekiel and Daniel

Daniel with the lions

INTRODUCTION

This chapter includes some of the most amazing visions recorded in the Hebrew Scriptures.

God's prophet, Ezekiel, speaks to the Jews, God's people, who had been exiled to Babylon from Jerusalem.

His striking visions of a caged lion, a crocodile, a valley of dry bones, and a rebuilt city of Jerusalem each carried its own special message.

Ezekiel taught the people that their much-loved city of Jerusalem had been destroyed because its leaders had turned away from God.

But these visions also gave the Jews hope as they languished in a strange land far from their city, their temple and, so it seemed, from their God.

Daniel was another sign of hope for the exiles. He and his three friends showed courage and faith: the friends in a blazing furnace and Daniel in a lions' den.

Model-making

SEEING JERUSALEM FROM BABYLON

Ezekiel lived with some of God's people who had been taken away as captives to Babylon just before Jerusalem was captured. Through Ezekiel, God told the Jews that Jerusalem would be destroyed.

A BRICK

God told Ezekiel to act out the siege of Jerusalem.

"Take a brick," God told Ezekiel. The obedient prophet soon understood.

"Draw a map of Jerusalem on the brick," God continued.

When Ezekiel was told to surround the city with an army, he used dozens of twigs and put them all around the brick.

Then he used many more twigs to represent the camps of the attacking army.

Then Ezekiel reached out for large, heavy logs. He put the logs next to the brick.

The Jews got the message. Jerusalem would be crushed.

THE SAD PEOPLE

"When the people of Jerusalem see their city being broken down, they will show how sad they are," God explained to Ezekiel. "They will replace their normal clothes with clothes made of rough cloth. Their bodies will shake with fear. Their faces will show how ashamed they are. Their hands will hang limply at their sides. Their voices will be like moaning doves. Their knees will wobble and give way under them."

Ezekiel chapter 4 verses 1 to 17, and chapter 7 verses 15 to 27

SILVER AND GOLD

Ezekiel was rather surprised when God then told him, "The people will throw all their gold and silver into the streets."

But then Ezekiel was quick to make the link between this gold and silver and the idols of gold and silver that the Jews had made and worshipped.

"Their gold will be like so much rubbish," said God angrily. "They loved their beautiful jewellery, and boasted about their golden idols. But they turned away from me. These evil people who are now attacking Jerusalem will take all its treasured jewels and gold and silver."

"And you, O mortal, take a brick and set it before you. On it portray a city, Jerusalem."

Ezekiel 4:1

Acting it out

God wanted the exiles in Babylon to understand that there was no hope for the people left behind in Jerusalem. They were refusing to trust God. So their city would be destroyed.

"Ezekiel," God commanded, "you're going to be an actor."

DURING THE DAY

God gave Ezekiel stage directions, "As the people watch you, Ezekiel, you are to pack your bags during the day. Pack everything you need for an exile — as much as you can carry in one large sack."

I did just as I was
commanded. I brought
out my baggage by day,
as baggage for exile.
Ezekiel 12:7

DURING THE NIGHT

"As soon as it is dark," continued God, "make a hole in the wall of your house. Push down enough stones to make a gap big enough to climb out through with your things. Then go through the hole, and walk out into the dark night."

AN EMPTY LAND

"Ezekiel," commanded God, "tell my people: 'Because you have not obeyed me I will make the land empty and desolate. There will be no rivers, no juicy grapes to pick. It will be like a desert.'"

And I will make the land desolate.

Ezekiel 15:8

Ezekiel and the symbols

The brick
When Ezekiel used a clay brick to represent the city of Jerusalem, he also took a sheet of iron and placed it between him and the brick. This showed that the siege of Jerusalem could not be broken.

Food in a besieged city
When Ezekiel was told to act out the siege of Jerusalem, he was told to store in a jar only the kind of food which would have been available in a besieged town: wheat, barley, beans, lentils, millet and spelt (Ezekiel 4:9).

The broken wall
When Ezekiel acted out an exile on the run from Jerusalem he dug through a wall. This was not the wall of Jerusalem, which was many feet thick, but the simple brick wall of his own house.

213

Is God fair?

Ezekiel told many stories.

214

THE FATHER

There were two men, a father and his son.

The father did what pleased God. He did not go up to the shrines of the idols in the mountains and worship them.

He was never unkind.

He never stole.

He shared his food with the hungry.

He gave clothes to those who didn't have any.

He does not oppress anyone, but . . . gives his bread to the hungry.

Ezekiel 18:7

THE SON

But his son went up to the shrines of the idols in the mountains and worshipped them.

He was often unkind.

He stole.

He mistreated the poor and the needy.

"MY DAD IS GOOD"

It won't help the son to say that he'll be all right in God's sight just because his dad was a good person. God says that each person is responsible for what he or she does.

With hooks they put him [a strong lion] in a cage, and brought him to the king of Babylon.

Ezekiel 19:9

Ezekiel chapter 18 verses 1 to 9, and chapter 19

Two lion cubs

Ezekiel told a story of the greatest of beasts, the lion. This sad tale reminded people of what had happened to their great country and their kings.

CUB NUMBER ONE

A lioness reared two cubs. The first cub became a strong lion that ate people. When the nations heard about the lion they dug a pit and put branches and leaves over it. The unsuspecting lion prowled around looking for the next meal, strode over the pit, and fell in. Then the lion was carted off to Egypt.

CUB NUMBER TWO

The lioness brought up her second cub to eat people, too. No town was safe. When the lion roared all the people shook with fear.

But this lion was caught, trapped, and put into a cage. The lion was paraded before the king of Babylon. The lion's roar was never heard again.

Lions and a lioness

Lioness
The lioness (Ezekiel 19:1) stands for the countries of Judah and Israel. The lioness may also represent Jerusalem, which was thought of as a mother to the kings of Judah and Israel.

The first cub
The first cub may represent King Jehoahaz who was taken off to Egypt (see Jeremiah 22:10-12). Jehoahaz ruled Judah for three months.

The second cub
The second cub may stand for King Jehoiachin, who was exiled to Babylon when King Nebuchadnezzar captured Jerusalem.

The great crocodile

216

Egypt thought of itself as one of the strongest nations in the world. But God had other ideas. God told Ezekiel to say that Egypt's days were numbered.

"You are like a great monster, like a mighty crocodile," God said about Egypt. "You are so proud," continued God , "that you dare to say: 'I made the River Nile. It is mine.'"

"I will drag you out of your rivers," warned God, "and feed you to the wild birds."

"I am against you, Pharaoh king of Egypt, the great dragon sprawling in the midst of its channels saying, 'My Nile is my own.'"

Ezekiel 29:3

CRY OVER EGYPT

"Ezekiel," ordered God, "say this funeral song about the king of Egypt.

Ezekiel chapter 29, and chapter 32 verses 1 to 4

217

This is who you are

'You are like a young lion among the nations.

You are like a crocodile in the seas.

You splash around in your streams. And you stir up the waters with your feet. You make the rivers muddy.'"

This is what will happen to you

"Egypt won't be great for ever," God assured Ezekiel. "Continue the funeral song:

'I will spread my net over you.
And I will use a large group of people
to pull you up in my net.
Then I will throw you on the land.
I will toss you into the open field.
I will let the birds of the sky rest on you.'" Ezekiel 32:2-4 ICB

And I will cause all the birds of the air to settle on you.

Ezekiel 32:4

Two messages

Someone who had escaped from Jerusalem came to me and said, "The city has fallen."

Ezekiel 33:21

THE SAD MESSAGE

"Ezekiel, tell the people why Jerusalem fell into enemy hands," said God.

Ezekiel had been a captive in Babylon for nearly thirteen years. A person who had escaped from Jerusalem came to him. "Jerusalem has been defeated," he told Ezekiel in great distress, as he held his head with his hands.

Ezekiel told the sad news to the rest of the captives in Babylon. "It went all so badly wrong for Jerusalem because her people listened to God's words with their ears but disobeyed God in their hearts and lives," explained Ezekiel.

Ezekiel chapter 33 verses 21 to 33, and chapter 36

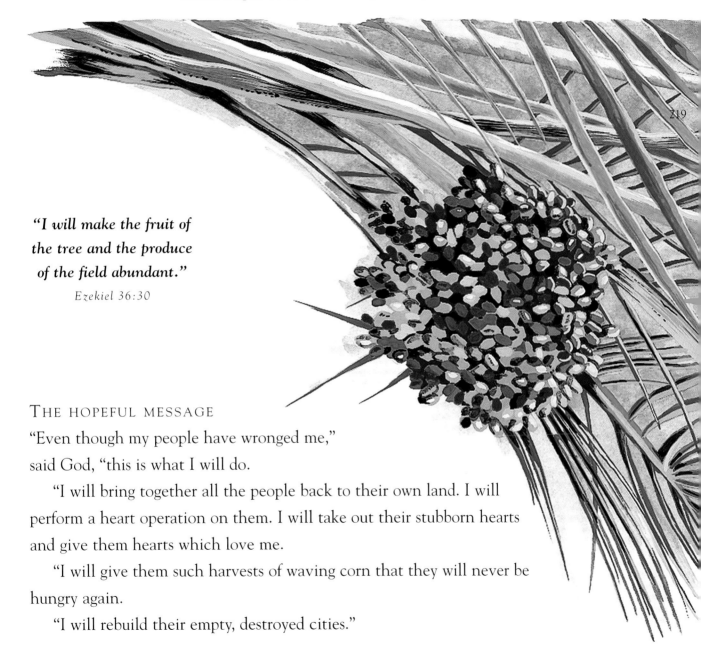

"I will make the fruit of the tree and the produce of the field abundant."

Ezekiel 36:30

THE HOPEFUL MESSAGE

"Even though my people have wronged me," said God, "this is what I will do.

"I will bring together all the people back to their own land. I will perform a heart operation on them. I will take out their stubborn hearts and give them hearts which love me.

"I will give them such harvests of waving corn that they will never be hungry again.

"I will rebuild their empty, destroyed cities."

Bones, bones, bones!

220

God gave me this mind-boggling vision. I just can't get it out of my mind. I was taken into the middle of a valley. As I looked around I gasped. It was full of bones. I could see ribs and skulls and all other parts of skeletons.

*The hand of the LORD
came upon me . . .
and set me down in
the middle of a valley;
it was full of bones.*

Ezekiel 37:1

Ezekiel chapter 37 verses 1 to 14, and chapter 48 verses 30 to 35

Can bones come alive?

God asked me, "Can these dry bones live?"

Of course, I had no idea, only God knew that.

Then God said, "Prophesy to these bones. Tell them: 'Dry bones, I will breath into you. You will come alive. You will have muscles, and flesh and skin.'"

Then there was a deafening rattle as all the bones came together. The wind blew with hurricane force. And then I saw them — people, not bones — all standing up, like an army.

"That, Ezekiel," explained God, "is what it will be like when I put my Spirit to live inside people."

And the name of the city from that time on shall be, The LORD is There.

Ezekiel 48:35

THE CITY'S NEW NAME

"Ezekiel, this is how you are to end your prophecy," explained God. "Tell my people that I can see a new city of Jerusalem. It will replace the smashed city. It will have twelve new strong gates, each one named after one of the tribes of Israel.

"I will give the city a new name. I will be there, among my people, so it will be called, 'God is There'."

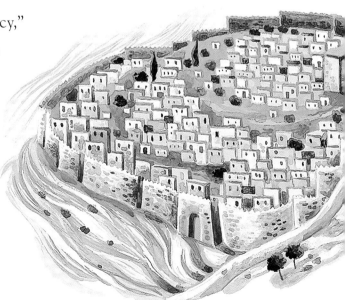

Daniel in exile

Daniel, a teenager, was one of the Jewish captives in Babylon. "I'm going to train some of those young Jewish exiles to serve in my court," announced Babylon's King Nebuchadnezzar. "Bring me healthy, clever, and good-looking ones."

THE BLAZING FURNACE

Daniel was selected, along with three of his friends. They thrived on a balanced vegetarian diet that they asked to eat, instead of the king's rich food and wine. God also helped them to be wise and quick to learn.

Even though they were in exile, Daniel's friends worshipped only God.

But in Babylon everyone else treated King Nebuchadnezzar as a god and worshipped him.

The king loved this. He had a giant gold statue made of himself. It was over 27 metres high and 2½ metres wide.

As soon as they heard the horns, flutes, zithers, harps and pipes playing, everyone bowed down and worshipped the statue.

. . . gave them vegetables.
Daniel 1:16

Everyone, that is,
except for Daniel's
friends Shadrach, Meshach
and Abednego.

They wouldn't worship
anyone but God. So the king
had them thrown into a
blazing furnace.

A FOURTH MYSTERIOUS FIGURE

King Nebuchadnezzar nearly fell off his throne
when he saw, not three, but four people in the
blazing furnace. "Look," exclaimed the King, "the four
of them are walking among the flames, but are not being
reduced to ashes. And look, the fourth one is like a god."

"Shadrach, Meshach and Abednego, come out of the
fire," commanded the perplexed king, "I see that the Most
High God, who you serve, has protected you."

King Nebuchadnezzar then made a new law: anyone who
insulted God would be punished.

*"But I see four men
unbound, walking in the
middle of the fire, and they
are not hurt."*

Daniel 3:25

Daniel chapter 6

A night with the lions

224

Daniel served the king of Babylon well, but he was hated by some of the Babylonian leaders. "He's a foreigner," they grumbled to each other, "and insists on worshipping his own special god . . . If only we could get rid of him."

Then they caught him — he was on his knees praying to God through his open window, which faced Jerusalem.

Then the king gave the command,
and Daniel was brought and
thrown into the den of lions.

Daniel 6:16

They hauled Daniel before the king. "We've caught Daniel praying to someone other than you, your Majesty. So he must go into the lions' den," the court officials said, hardly able to hide their delight.

Reluctantly, the king had to agree. But that night God sent angels to shut the lions' mouths. So the lions did not eat Daniel for supper.

In the morning the king rushed to the den to see if Daniel was still alive. Servants hauled Daniel out, safe and well. Daniel had trusted God, and God had protected Daniel.

Chapter 14: From the Bible books of Hosea, Amos, Micah, Jonah, Obadiah, Habakkuk, Zechariah and Malachi

Jonah's fishy tale

INTRODUCTION

This chapter gives glimpses into the "minor prophets" of the Hebrew Scriptures. Included are the famous Jonah, always a favourite, and Hosea, Amos, Micah, Obadiah, Habakkuk, Zechariah and Malachi.

Prophets used everyday things to teach God's people. There are weeds in Hosea, a lion in Amos, a high-flying eagle in Obadiah, ploughs in Micah, a strange stone in Zechariah, and grapes in Malachi.

Using these objects, the prophets taught people to be faithful and to trust God.

These prophets preached in three hard times: just before Babylon's army destroyed Jerusalem, while God's people were captives in Babylon, and after people went back to rebuild their ruined country. The prophets helped people understand why these things had happened and gave them hope.

Two messages from Hosea

"Nettles shall possess their precious things of silver; thorns shall be in their tents."

Hosea 9:6

WEEDS

Hosea told the people of Israel, "Because you have not trusted God, you will be punished. You won't have enough grain to feed yourselves. You won't have enough wine to drink.

"Even if you are not killed, the Egyptians will capture you.

"Your land will be a total disaster. It will be overgrown with weeds. Your treasures of silver will be taken over by weeds, and thorns will overrun your tents."

Hosea chapter 9 verses 1 to 9, and chapter 13 verses 1 to 3

IDOLS

Hosea tried to warn the people that terrible things would happen if they didn't start listening to and trusting God:

"You have sinned against God in terrible ways.

"You have made idols out of silver. Then you have worshipped these idols instead of worshipping God.

"These idols may have looked beautiful to you because they were made by skilled artists, but in God's sight, they were hideous."

"You even pay more attention to these idols than you do to God.

"You show your love and respect for these idols by actually kissing them!"

The Minor Prophets

The book of Hosea is the first of the last 12 books of the Hebrew Scriptures. These were first called "the minor prophets" in the late fourth century.

The 12 prophetic books are:
Hosea, Joel, Amos, Obadiah, Jonah, Micah, Nahum, Habakkuk, Zephaniah, Haggai, Zechariah, and Malachi.

Before the birth of Jesus, these 12 books were joined together and known as "the Twelve".

They are called "minor" prophets, not because they are unimportant, but because they are so much shorter than the "major" prophecies of Isaiah, Jeremiah, and Ezekiel.

"The Twelve" have only 67 chapters in total, while the book of Isaiah alone has 66 chapters.

They . . . make a cast image for themselves, idols of silver made according to their understanding.

Hosea 13:2

227

Insects invade

VARIETIES OF LOCUSTS

Joel pictures the land of Judah being invaded by a massive invasion of locusts:

"What the cutting locusts have not eaten,
the swarming locusts have eaten,
And what the swarming locusts have left,
the hopping locusts have eaten.
And what the hopping locusts have left,
the destroying locusts have eaten." Joel 1:4 ICB

LIKE AN ARMY

Joel continues:

"A powerful nation has come into my land.
It has too many soldiers to count.
It has teeth like a lion.
And it has fangs like a female lion.
The army has eaten my grapevines.
It has destroyed my fig trees.
It has eaten the bark off my trees
and left the branches white." Joel 1:6-7 ICB

Locusts

Their appetite

The books of Joel, Amos, and Nahum all mention locusts. They are seen as God punishing people and are given as a warning, to help people return to God.

Locusts, a large variety of grasshopper, often collect together and move around in a million-strong swarm.

They eat every kind of vegetation they can get their teeth into. They can strip fields, trees and grasslands with devastating results.

Their method of travel

Some locusts fly like gliders. They use their wings to launch themselves into the sky and then allow the wind to carry them along. They can fly, or sail along, like this for up to 100 miles.

At night, they land in trees or grasses. All night long they gobble up all the plant life. In the morning they take off again.

Because of the great destruction they caused, the Romans called locusts, "burners of the land".

LOOK AT THE LAND

Joel then speaks about the farmers:

"The fields are ruined.

Even the ground is dried up.

The grain is destroyed.

The new wine is dried up.

And the olive oil runs out.

Be sad, farmers.

Cry loudly, you who grow grapes.

Cry for the wheat and the barley.

Cry because the harvest in the field is lost!"

Joel 1:10-11 ICB

What the cutting locusts have not eaten, the swarming locusts have eaten.

Joel 1:4

Be sad, farmers. Cry loudly, you who grow grapes.

Joel 1:11 ICB

230

Amos speaks up against Israel

The lion has roared!

Amos 3:8

THE LION'S ROAR

God's prophet, Amos, a shepherd from Tekoa in Judah, spoke against the people who lived in the country of Israel.

"Don't you know what it means when you hear the lion's roar?" he asked God's people who were not trusting in God. "It means that he has sprung on his prey," continued Amos, "he has caught his next meal. God's voice of judgment on your sins is like that."

The LORD said to me, "Amos, what do you see?" And I said, "A plumb-line."

Amos 7:8

THE PLUMB LINE

"You are meant to be God's faithful people, built like a straight building," boomed Amos. "But God's plumb line will show how crooked you are."

Amos chapter 3 verses 1 to 8, and chapter 5 verse 21 to chapter 7 verse 9

A plumb line

Why it is used
A plumb line has been used by builders since ancient times to make sure that the wall which they are building goes straight up.

How it was made
The plumb line had three parts. At the base was a lead weight in the shape of an upside-down cone.

At the top was a wooden rod, the same width as the cone. The weight and rod were linked by a cord.

How it is used
A builder places the wooden rod against the top edge of the top level of stones or bricks of the wall. If the wall is upright and true, the side of the lead weight just touches the lowest line of bricks.

Alas for those who lie on beds of ivory, and lounge on their couches.

Amos 6:4

LET JUSTICE ROLL

Amos spoke out against those who were unfair to the poor. "God says, 'I hate your extravagant worship and noisy hymns. Instead, let justice roll down like a river that never runs dry.'"

Amos criticized people who lived in the lap of luxury but didn't care what was happening to their country. "You think nothing can harm you," Amos protested. "You loll about on expensive couches feasting on the finest food and drink. And you forget about God."

231

Jonah is rescued

**But Jonah set out to flee to Tarshish
from the presence of the LORD.**

Jonah 1:3

Jonah did not like God's idea of going to and preaching to the wicked people of
Nineveh. So he went off in the opposite direction and caught a boat to Tarshish.

But Jonah soon learned that it was not that easy to escape from carrying out God's
orders.

"We're about to sink," yelled the desperate captain of the ship. "Quick, before the
forty foot waves sink the boat, throw our precious cargo overboard." "That will make
the boat lighter and help us to keep afloat," thought the experienced sailor.

JONAH WAKES UP

The captain found that Jonah had been asleep all this time. "Get up, and pray to your God," shouted the captain in Jonah's ear as he shook him.

Jonah confessed that this storm was because he was running away from God.

THE RESCUE

Reluctantly, the sailors threw Jonah overboard, as he had suggested.

At once the sea became calm, the wind died down and the rain stopped.

The tough sailors rubbed their eyes in disbelief. The largest fish they had ever seen swam along, opened its mouth, and swallowed Jonah whole.

Inside the massive fish's stomach Jonah thanked God that he had been rescued. Three days later the fished coughed him up, just by some dry land, safe and sound, but very smelly.

Then the LORD spoke to the fish, and it spewed Jonah out upon the dry land.

Jonah 2:10

Micah chapter 3 verses 1 to chapter 4 verse 5, and chapter 6 verses 6 to 8

Micah and war

234

WARNING FOR LEADERS

"You leaders and rich people crush the poor," said the prophet Micah. "You lie and cheat."

"Rich people bribe the judges to get their own way," he continued. "That isn't justice!"

"As for you prophets," Micah raged, "if people pay you, you tell them what they want to hear. That isn't speaking God's truth!"

PEACE WILL COME

Micah knew his nation was in big trouble. But he also knew that some day there would be peace. "The time will come when we won't have wars to settle our arguments. God will help countries make peace treaties. People won't need weapons; they will make ploughs out of their swords and gardening tools from their spears. No one will be taught how to fight. Everyone will sit free of fear under their grape vines.

WHAT DOES GOD WANT?

The people who heard Micah wondered what to do. "If we have a nice worship service, maybe God will be pleased," they said.

"No," said Micah. "This is what God wants, only this: do what is just, love tenderly, and walk humbly with God."

But they shall all sit
under their own vines
and under their own fig
trees, and no one shall
make them afraid.

Micah 4:4

Habakkuk's question

236

"Why," Habakkuk asked God, "does all the evil the people of Judah are doing go unpunished?"

GOD'S ANSWER

"They will be punished," God replied.

"This is what will happen," explained God. "The Babylonians will punish Judah.

"I will use the Babylonian people to punish the evil people.

The Babylonians are cruel and powerful fighters.

. . . Their horses are faster than leopards and more cruel than wolves at sunset.

*"Their horses
are swifter than
leopards."*

Habakkuk 1:8

Habakkuk chapter 1 verses 1 to 8, and chapter 3 verses 1 to 19

Their horse soldiers attack quickly.

They come from places that are far away.

They attack quickly, like an eagle swooping down for food." Habakkuk 1:6, 8 ICB

HABAKKUK'S PRAYER

Habakkuk faces sadness and disaster, but shows trust and faith in God, in this prayer:

"Fig trees may not grow figs.

There may be no grapes on the vines.

There may be no olives growing on the trees.

There may be no food growing in the fields.

There may be no sheep in the pens.

There may be no cattle in the barns.

But I will still be glad in the Lord.

I will rejoice in God my Saviour.

The Lord God gives me my strength."

Habakkuk 3:17, 18 ICB

There may be no grapes on the vines.

Habakkuk 3:17 ICB

Zechariah's vision of a stone

238

God gave Zechariah a vivid vision to show how God would forgive the people of Israel.

"I saw Joshua, in my vision," recounted Zechariah. "He was all dressed up in dirty clothes. 'Take off your filthy clothes, Joshua,' an angel ordered. 'See,' explained the angel, 'I have taken away your sin. Now put on these new clothes I am giving you. And put a clean turban on your head.'

"'I am now placing a special stone in front of you,' continued the angel. 'It has seven sides with a special message written on it. In one day I will take away the sin of this land.'

"'This is how I will bless you,' promised the angel. 'When the time comes, you will each invite your neighbour to join you. And you will sit together under your vine and fig tree.'"

"For on the stone that I have set before Joshua, on a single stone with seven facets . . . "

Zechariah 3:9

Zechariah chapter 3 verses 1 to 10, and chapter 8 verses 1 to 23

239

Many people and strong nations shall come to seek the LORD of Hosts.

Zechariah 8:22

GOD'S BLESSING SPREADS

Zechariah predicted the time when many people from powerful nations would go to Jerusalem. This time it would not be to capture the city, but to be blessed by God.

"This is what God says," Zechariah continued:

"When it happens, people will come from many different countries, speaking many different languages. They will grab hold of a Jew's clothes and beg, 'Take us with you. We know God is with you.'"

Malachi chapter 3 verses 6 to 12

Blessed by God

Malachi, in the last book in the Hebrew Scriptures, looks forward to the time when God will bless his people. By this time, many of the Jews had gone back to live in Jerusalem.

"Okay, people of Judah," started Malachi, "I know that you have rebuilt God's temple.

240

"I will . . . open the windows of heaven for you and pour down for you an overflowing blessing."

Malachi 3:10

But you should be sharing more of what you have — you should give ten per cent of your income. Here is God's promise to you if you do this: 'I will open the windows of heaven for you. I will pour out more blessings than you have room for. I will stop the insects so they won't eat your crops. The grapes won't fall from your vines before they are ready to pick.'"

Malachi 3:10-11 ICB

NEW TESTAMENT

Chapter 15: From the Bible books of Matthew, Mark and Luke

Jesus the healer

INTRODUCTION

This first chapter from the New Testament is all about the life of Jesus.

It starts with stories about Jesus' birth and childhood. It then moves on to the time when he was about 30 years old. Jesus chose some special helpers. Large crowds of people came to listen to his stories, such as the parables of the farmer and the seed, which were remembered long after he told them.

Jesus became a powerful healer of adults as well as children. He healed a man with a crippled hand. He also brought a 12-year-old girl back to life.

We are introduced to two very different sisters, Mary and Martha, and to other followers and friends of Jesus.

This book ends with the story about the day when Jesus' face shone like the sun.

Two babies to be born

When Elizabeth heard Mary's greeting, the child leapt in her womb. And Elizabeth was filled with the Holy Spirit.

Luke 1:41

A SURPRISE BABY

Mary had no idea that she was going to be Jesus' mother until an angel said to her, "Don't be afraid, Mary, because God is pleased with you. Listen! You will give birth to a son, and you will name him Jesus."

ELIZABETH'S BABY

Mary visited her relative Elizabeth, who was expecting a baby. "My baby's going to be a miracle baby, Mary," Elizabeth explained. "I am so old. Only God could give me a baby at my time of life."

MARY'S BABY

Mary had astonishing news of her own. "Elizabeth, I'm going to have a baby too," Mary said joyfully. "He will be called Son of the Most High and Son of God. He is going to be a holy baby."

Luke chapter 1 verse 5 to chapter 2 verse 20

Jesus is born

MARY'S SONG

Mary sang about what God had done:

My spirit dances; God is magnificent.

God cares deeply about people the world

doesn't see.

God strengthens those who are weak.

He lifts up the little ones, but humbles the proud.

He fills the hungry and sends the rich away

empty.

A HUMBLE BIRTH

Mary and Joseph arrived in Bethlehem just before

Jesus' birth. But there were no rooms left in the

inn. So Jesus was born in a stable. Joseph put clean

straw in a box where animals are fed and Mary

gently placed the new-born baby Jesus on the straw.

That night, angels told the news about the birth

to shepherds up in the hills. "Glory to God and

peace on earth," sang the angels. The shepherds

rushed to the stable to worship Jesus.

And she gave birth to her firstborn son and wrapped him in bands of cloth, and laid him in a manger.

Luke 2:7

243

The child, Jesus

SIMEON AND ANNA MEET JESUS

Mary and Joseph took Jesus to the temple to give a thank-you gift to God. There, they met an old man named Simeon, who loved God. Simeon cuddled baby Jesus and whispered a prayer: "Thank you, God. Now I can die in peace."

"This baby will change the future of many people," Simeon told Mary and Joseph.

They were just as surprised by Anna, the old temple prophet. "Praise God!" Anna exclaimed. Anna told everyone who would listen who this baby was.

VISITING MAGI

Wise men from the east came looking for Jesus. They made the mistake of asking King Herod for directions to the new king. Jealous Herod hatched a plot to kill the child. The wise men came to Bethlehem with gifts of gold, frankincense and myrrh. An angel warned Joseph of Herod's evil plot and Jesus, Mary and Joseph escaped just in time.

JESUS VISITS THE TEMPLE

When Jesus was twelve, his family went to Jerusalem for the Passover. On the way home, Mary and Joseph couldn't find Jesus. He was still in the temple in Jerusalem. "I had to be in my Father's house," he explained.

Luke chapter 2 verses 22 to 52, and Mark chapter 1 verses 1 to 11

The baptism of Jesus

JOHN BAPTIZES
JESUS

John preached,
"Change your ways!
Make way for God!"

"What should we
do?" people asked.

"Share what you
have. Be fair. Don't be
bullies," was John's message.

If people really had a
change of heart, John
baptized them in the Jordan
River.

John baptized Jesus. After
Jesus came out of the water,
the Spirit came down like a
dove. A voice said, "You are
my child, my beloved."

*And the Holy Spirit
descended upon him in
bodily form, like a dove.*

Luke 3:22

Four fishers

246

ANDREW AND PETER

As Jesus walked along the edge of the shoreline of Lake Galilee he saw two pairs of brothers. The first two were Andrew and Peter. These young, strong, tanned fishermen were busily throwing their net into the water looking for another catch of fish.

Jesus said to them, "Come and follow me. You will no longer catch fish, you will catch people. I will make you fishers for people."

At once, Andrew and Peter dropped their nets and followed Jesus.

JAMES AND JOHN

A little further along Lake Galilee Jesus saw the second pair of brothers. James and John were in their family fishing boat with their father Zebedee.

"James and John, come and follow me," Jesus called.

At once they left their father and followed Jesus.

When Jesus was walking by Lake Galilee, he saw Simon and Simon's brother, Andrew.

Mark 1:16 ICB

Matthew chapter 10 verses 2 to 4, and Luke chapter 8 verses 1 to 3

Followers of Jesus

FRIENDS AND APOSTLES

Jesus had many followers, friends and helpers. Twelve of his disciples were called apostles, that is, people who were specially chosen to help Jesus in his ministry. Some famous apostles were: Simon (also called Peter), James, John, Thomas, Matthew, and Andrew. Judas was one of Jesus' apostles. How terrible it was that Judas betrayed Jesus.

WOMEN TRAVEL WITH JESUS

Jesus went to many cities and villages telling good news about God. His twelve disciples went with him, and some women that Jesus had healed. These included Mary Magdalene, Joanna, Suzanna. The women used their own money to help Jesus.

The twelve were with him, as well as some women who had been cured.

Luke 8:1-2

Disciples and apostles

247

The word "disciple" means "learner". When Jesus started out, he chose twelve disciples — "the Twelve" — to be with him. As time passed, many people became followers of Jesus, but a lot dropped away when the going got tough.

After a night of prayer, Jesus summoned his followers. He called out "the Twelve" and named them "apostles" (Luke 6:12-16). They were his representatives.

The farmer and the seed

JESUS TELLS A STORY

A farmer planted seeds.

Some seeds fell on the path, where the birds ate them.

Some seeds fell on the rocks. The plants had no roots, so they withered in the sun.

Some seeds fell among weeds and were choked out.

But some seeds landed in good soil, where they grew well and produced a lot of grain.

FOUR TYPES OF LISTENERS

"The farmer," explained Jesus, "is like a person who shares God's teaching.

"The four types of soil stand for four types of people who listen to God's teaching.

"The path is like people who let Satan snatch God's teaching from their minds.

"The rocky soil is like those people who are full of joy at first. But as soon as troubles come along, they collapse.

"The seeds overgrown with weeds are like people who accept God's teaching. But, later, their worries, their love of money, and their longing for everything else in life, squeezes out God's teaching.

"But the good soil is like listeners who welcome God's

teaching into their lives and follow it. They grow and grow in goodness and love."

"Other seed fell into good soil and brought forth grain."

Mark 4:8

They watched him to see whether he would cure him on the sabbath.

Mark 3:2

A man with a crippled hand

As Jesus went into the synagogue he at once saw a man who had a crippled hand.

"What would Jesus do?" some people thought to themselves. "Jesus won't heal him, as it is against the law to heal anyone on the Sabbath," they reckoned.

Jesus could read their minds. "Tell me, is it right to do good or to do evil on the Sabbath?"

They were dumbfounded and gave no answer.

Jesus said to the crippled man, "Let me look at your hand." To everyone's great surprise, the man moved his hand and was healed.

But the Pharisees were furious. They left to hatch a plot to kill Jesus.

Matthew chapter 8 verses 28 to 34

Jesus heals two men

DEMONS

There were two men who nobody wanted to meet.
They lived all by themselves in caves which were used
to bury dead people. Anybody who came near them
was attacked. Worst of all — they were full of demons.

But they came to meet Jesus. The demons in the
two men spoke to Jesus: "What do you want to do
with us, Son of God? Have you come to punish us?"

PIGS

"If you make us leave these two men," continued the
demons, "let us go into these pigs."

Jesus commanded them with a single word: "Go!"

The demons left the men and went into the pigs.
The pigs rushed down the hill into a lake where they were
drowned.

The two men felt well and happy and smiled broadly as
they thanked Jesus for all he had done for them.

They were so fierce that no one could pass that way.

Matthew 8:28

Jesus heals a woman

TWELVE YEARS OF ILLNESS

A certain poor woman had been ill for twelve long years. When she first felt sick, she went immediately to the doctor, but she didn't get any better. So she went to a second doctor, but still was not better. She tried every doctor in town, but no one could help her. Finally, she had no money left because she had spent all her savings on doctors' fees and medicines. Worst of all, no one wanted to go near her because of her illness.

THE WOMAN'S TOUCH

One day the woman heard about a young man who preached and healed people. So she joined the crowd and listened

She had heard about Jesus, and came up behind him in the crowd and touched his cloak.

Mark 5:27

to the man, who was Jesus. Then she edged her way closer and closer to Jesus, until he was just in front of her.

Then she did it. She stretched out her hand and touched Jesus' coat. She was sure nobody would notice. But as she did this she was completely better. She knew Jesus had healed her.

JESUS' QUESTION

As the woman touched him, Jesus felt power leave him. He stopped walking and turned round. "Who touched me?" he asked.

"Isn't that a bit of a silly question?" suggested someone. "There are so many people bumping into you all the time, how can you ask, 'Who touched me?'"

But Jesus was not put off. He continued to look around to find the person who had touched him. The woman knew that she had been discovered. Trembling, she came up to Jesus, bowed low before him, and said, "It was me." And she told Jesus why she had done it.

A HAPPY ENDING

But she didn't need to be afraid. Jesus was not angry with her. "Dear woman," Jesus said to her gently, as he took her hand and helped her to stand upright, "you are well because you trusted in God. You will suffer no more. Go in peace."

Jesus brings a girl back to life

254

Jairus was a very important person, the top man in his synagogue. He approached Jesus; he was desperate.

"Jesus," he said as he bowed down low, "my daughter has just died. But I know that if you touch her, she will be well."

JESUS' TOUCH

When Jesus arrived at the dead girl's home he said, "She isn't dead, she's only sleeping." He took her hand in his hand and said, "Little girl, get up." She stood up. And everyone in her village heard about this miracle.

Peter, James and John
Peter, James and John were Jesus' closest friends. Jesus took them, and only them, with him at some special times.

"Jesus let only Peter, James, and John the brother of James go with him to Jairus's house" (Mark 5:37 ICB).

Jesus took these three apostles with him up a mountain where he was changed and his clothes became shining white (Mark 9:2-8).

In the Garden of Gethsemane, only Peter, James, and John were allowed to be close to Jesus as he prayed.

But when the crowd had been put outside, he went in and took her by the hand, and the girl got up.

Matthew 9:25

Mary and Martha

MARTHA'S GRUMBLING

Mary and Martha might have been sisters, but they could not have been more different. They and their brother Lazarus were good friends with Jesus. They often put Jesus up for the night and gave him a meal. Their home at Bethany was just a few miles from Jerusalem.

"Won't anybody help me?" muttered Martha. "Why does Mary always sit and talk with Jesus, leaving me to do all the cooking!"

"Martha, Martha," replied Jesus soothingly, "you are getting worried and upset about too many things. Only one thing is important. Mary has chosen the right thing, and it will never be taken away from her" (Luke 10:42 ICB).

But Martha was distracted by her many tasks; so she came to him and asked, "Lord, do you not care that my sister has left me to do all the work?"

Luke 10:40

Everything changes

GOD IS HERE

"God's time is not far off in the future," said Jesus to his close friends. They didn't get it. "God's time is right now. God's power is with us right now," Jesus explained.

A few days later, they got to see first hand what Jesus meant.

UP THE MOUNTAIN

Jesus took his closest friends up a mountain. Before their very eyes, Jesus changed. His clothes shone as though they had been dipped in dazzling paint. Then they saw Moses and Elijah talking to Jesus.

"What should we do?" exclaimed Peter in terror. "We should make a shelter for each of them." He didn't know what he was talking about.

A cloud drifted low over the mountain and they couldn't see past the end of their noses. A voice from the cloud said, "This is my Son, the Beloved. Listen to him."

The clouds lifted, and they saw only Jesus standing there. They puzzled over what this could possibly mean.

And from the cloud there came a voice, "This is my Son, the Beloved; listen to him."

Mark 9:7

NEW TESTAMENT

Chapter 16: From the Bible books of Matthew, John and Acts

Jesus is betrayed

INTRODUCTION

In this chapter, we hear more about the teaching of Jesus.

We also read about the last meal Jesus had with his followers and the mysterious words he said about his body and blood being bread and wine.

Then we read about the moment when Judas left the other followers of Jesus. He went out into the night to betray Jesus and hand him over to people who wanted Jesus killed.

We hear how Jesus died on the cross and came alive again three days later.

Then, we learn that Jesus' disciples received the Holy Spirit at the Feast of Pentecost.

There are a number of "firsts" in this chapter: the first recorded healing by Jesus' followers after Jesus was killed; the first Christian martyr; the first person brought back from the dead by a disciple of Jesus; and the first African to become a follower of Jesus.

One lost sheep

*"And if he finds it, truly
I tell you, he rejoices
over it more than over
the ninety-nine that
never went astray."*

Matthew 18:13

Jesus told this story about a caring shepherd who had 100 sheep.

One day one of the 100 sheep decided to go off on its own. It got lost and couldn't find its way back to the other 99 sheep. It was scared that it might be eaten by a lion, or gobbled up by a bear.

Then the sheep saw its best friend, the loving shepherd. The shepherd had left the other 99 sheep just to come looking for the lost sheep. The shepherd knew how tired and weak and hungry the lost sheep had become. He was so relieved and happy to find the little sheep that he lifted it gently on to his shoulders and carried it back to the safety of the sheepfold.

Jesus ended this story by saying: "God does not want any of his little children to be lost."

Matthew chapter 18 verses 10 to 14, and Luke chapter 15 verses 8 to 10

One lost coin

LOOKING IN THE CORNERS

Jesus told a story about a woman who had ten silver coins but lost one.

"Now, what have I done with that tenth silver coin?" she asked herself. "I'm always putting things down and forgetting where I've put them. I don't know how I could have lost that coin."

"There's nothing for it, I'll have to look for it until I find it."

She started by lighting her oil lamp. Then she carefully swept her dusty floor. She looked in one corner of the room, then in the second corner, then in the third corner, but she found no coin. Getting desperate she swept the fourth corner. And there it was!

"I'VE FOUND IT!"

"Wonderful," the woman shouted out. She rushed to her friends and neighbours: "Be happy with me — I've found the coin I lost."

Jesus ended this parable with the words: "In the same way, there is joy before the angels of God over one sinner who repents."

> *"Rejoice with me, for I have found the coin that I had lost."*
>
> Luke 15:9

One silver coin

The woman in Jesus' story may have lost a very precious thing. Her lost silver coin might have been equivalent to an engagement ring. If it was one of the ten silver coins which formed a headdress, it may have been part of her dowry.

The coin she lost was a drachma, a Greek coin worth a day's wages.

Looking for the coin may have been no easy matter, because her house probably had no windows. So the woman would have crawled on her hands and knees, while holding her oil lamp and feeling for the coin on her earthen floor.

259

Matthew chapter 10 verses 37 to 42, and chapter 19 verses 13 to 15

The "whoevers"

Jesus taught the people and said:

"Whoever does not take up a cross and follow me is not worthy of me."

"Whoever tries to hold on to their life will lose true life."

"Whoever helps one of these little ones will get their reward even if they only give a cup of cold water."

People brought children to Jesus for him to bless them. Some disciples tried to keep the children away. Jesus said, "Whoever doesn't welcome God's realm like a little child will never enter it. God's reign belongs to children." Then Jesus blessed them.

"Whoever gives even a cup of cold water to one of these little ones in the name of a disciple — truly I tell you, none of these will lose their reward."

Matthew 10:42

260

John chapter 15 verses 1 to 9, and Matthew chapter 6 verses 8 to 13

Jesus is like a vine

"I AM THE TRUE VINE"

Jesus said to the disciples:

"I am the vine; God is the gardener. God cuts off branches that don't produce fruit and trims branches that produce fruit. I am the vine, and you are the branches. Those with me produce much fruit."

A SPECIAL PRAYER

Jesus said, "Pray like this:

Our Father, Holy One,

May your time come, may your will be done in earth as in heaven.

Give us the bread we need for today.

Forgive our debts as we have forgiven the debts of others.

Keep us safe always."

I am the vine, you are the branches.
Those who abide in me and I in them
bear much fruit.

John 15:5

Vines

261

In the Hebrew Scriptures, vines, which bear juicy grapes for eating and for wine-making, represent God's people Israel. They were thought of as being God's vine. A bunch of grapes was carved on the outside of most synagogues.

But Israel did not obey God. "How then did you turn into a wild vine that grows bad fruit?" asked Jeremiah (Jeremiah 2:21 ICB).

Jesus the true vine
All who obey Jesus are like branches on a fruitful vine, tended by God.

The special meal

262

PASSOVER

It was Passover, the festival when Jews remember how God freed the Israelites from slavery in Egypt. On Thursday evening, Jesus planned a Passover meal with his friends.

BREAD

At the meal, Jesus did something his friends remembered after he was dead. It helped them to understand what happened later.

While they were eating supper, Jesus took some bread. He thanked God for it and broke it. Then he gave it to his followers. He said, "Take this bread and eat. This bread is my body."

WINE

Then Jesus took a goblet of wine, thanked God and gave it to the followers. Jesus said, "Drink this. This is my blood, which is poured out for many to forgive sins."

ONE MORE CLUE

Jesus gave his followers one more clue by talking about heaven. He said, "I will not drink any more wine until I drink it new with you in God's realm."

Judas the betrayer

JESUS' SOLEMN ANNOUNCEMENT

Jesus was eating the last meal he would have with his disciples. "One of you is going to turn against me," Jesus said sadly.

His friends looked at each other with dismay. "Who's he talking about?" they whispered to each other.

The disciple whom Jesus specially loved was sitting next to Jesus. So Peter nodded to him and said, "Ask Jesus who he is talking about."

The disciple leaned over to Jesus and asked, "Who is going to betray you, Lord?"

Jesus said, "The person I give this bread to is the one." Jesus then took a piece of bread, dipped it in a dish, and gave it to Judas.

JUDAS GOES INTO THE NIGHT

Judas took the bread. Immediately, he left the table and went out. It was night.

So, after receiving the piece of bread, he immediately went out. And it was night.

John 13:30

Jesus dies, but comes back to life

264

THE SOLDIERS

The soldiers arrested Jesus. Jesus was put on trial and whipped. The Roman soldiers nailed Jesus to the cross. Some of Jesus' friends, including Peter, ran away in fear, but Mary Magdalene and the other women stayed.

JESUS LOVES TO THE END

Jesus saw his mother, Mary, and John, at the foot of his cross.

Jesus said to Mary, "Here is your son." To John, Jesus said, "Here is your mother." So John took Mary to live in his home.

JESUS DIES

A little later, Jesus said in a clear, loud voice, "It is finished." He bowed his head and died.

Mary Magdalene came to the tomb and saw that the stone had been removed from the tomb.

John 20:1

JESUS IS BURIED

A man named Joseph, from Arimathea, and a leading rabbi named Nicodemus took the body of Jesus, wrapped it and laid it in a tomb. This was the usual way Jews buried their dead.

JESUS' TOMB IS EMPTY

Just before dawn Mary Magdalene went to Jesus' tomb. Mary saw that the large stone had been mysteriously rolled away. She looked in the tomb. Jesus' body was gone! As Mary stood crying she heard a voice say, "Mary." It was Jesus! Mary rushed off to tell the others, "I have seen Jesus!"

All of them were filled with the Holy Spirit.

Acts 2:4

Acts chapter 1 verses 8 to 26 and chapter 2 verses 1 to 13

The Holy Spirit comes

WAITING

Jesus' disciples had seen the risen Lord Jesus many times after he had come alive. For forty days they listened to his every word. "Don't leave Jerusalem," he told them. "Wait here until you receive the Holy Spirit."

WIND, FIRE, AND DIFFERENT LANGUAGES

So the disciples waited. Then, on the day of Pentecost, it happened.

They heard a strange noise, like a mighty wind blowing.

They saw flames of fire — one flame of fire on top of each person.

They spoke in a variety of languages.

POWER FROM GOD

The Holy Spirit had arrived to give Jesus' followers power from God. In the strength of this power they preached and healed people.

Peter heals a man

THE BEAUTIFUL GATE

It was nearly three o'clock. Peter and John were on their way to pray at the temple. As they came to the temple gate called Beautiful Gate, they saw a man sitting on the ground — he had never been able to walk.

"STAND UP AND WALK!"

Peter stretched out his hand and took hold of the man's right hand and helped him stand up. At once the man's ankles and feet were made strong. He went into the temple, jumping for joy and giving thanks to God for this wonderful miracle.

When he saw Peter and John about to go into the temple, he asked them for alms.

Acts 3:3

The first Christian martyr

*But they covered their ears, and
with a loud shout all rushed
together against him.*

Acts 7:57

ARRESTED FOR SERVING GOD

After Jesus' death, his
followers carried on his
work. They taught, cared
for the poor, healed
people, and shared
whatever they had
with each other.
Stephen had
been given special power
by God. Everywhere he went, he healed people and
performed amazing miracles.

Jealous Jews were furious. "We'll take him on," they said to
each other. And they argued against him. But the more they

argued, the more everyone else saw how wise Stephen was.

That was the last straw. They grabbed Stephen and brought him before the Jewish leaders. "We charge the accused with saying that Jesus will change the things Moses has taught us. He even said that Jesus of Nazareth will destroy the temple."

All eyes were on Stephen. As he began his defence, everyone saw that his face was like that of an angel.

STEPHEN'S DEFENCE
Stephen started to accuse his accusers. "You stubborn Jewish leaders!" said Stephen. "You have not given your hearts to God! You are always against what the Holy Spirit is trying to tell you" (Acts 7:51, 52 ICB).

STEPHEN IS STONED
The Jewish leaders had had enough. They ground their teeth in anger. They went for Stephen, dragged him outside the walls of Jerusalem, and threw rocks and large stones at him. Stephen did not try to defend himself, but just prayed, "Jesus, receive my spirit!" One stone hit Stephen on the forehead and he fell to his knees. Stephen summoned up all his remaining strength for a last prayer, "Lord, do not hold this sin against them!"

Philip and the Ethiopian

270

AN ETHIOPIAN OFFICIAL

Philip had a vision of an angel urging him to go to a road in the wilderness.

There he saw a magnificent chariot. It belonged to an Ethiopian, a high official in the queen's court. In fact, this man was so important he was in charge of all the queen's money. The Ethiopian had come to Jerusalem to worship and was returning home.

PHILIP TALKS ABOUT JESUS

Philip went over to the chariot and walked along beside it. The Ethiopian was reading the scroll of the prophet Isaiah. "Do you understand it?" Philip asked.

"How can I?" replied the Ethiopian. "I don't have anyone to teach me."

Philip explained that the prophet Isaiah was talking about a person God would send to save God's people. Then Philip told the Ethiopian all about Jesus.

A NEW FOLLOWER

The Ethiopian believed instantly. "I want to become a follower of Jesus," he declared. When they came to some water he commanded the chariot to stop and Philip baptized him right on the spot.

Peter and Dorcas

The followers of Jesus performed many miracles after they received the Holy Spirit. They were very upset when one of them, a lady called Dorcas, died.

Peter went to the upstairs room where she lay.

When he managed to empty the room of all the sad people he kneeled and prayed. Then he turned towards Dorcas' body and said, "Dorcas, stand up!" Her eyes opened. Peter held out his hand, and helped her to her feet.

All the widows stood beside him, weeping and showing tunics and other clothing that Dorcas had made while she was with them.

Acts 9:39

Living for God

272

LIVE IN PEACE

Jesus' followers continued to spread the good news and heal people. They impressed everyone around them with the love and care they showed. Paul summed up their attitude in advice he gave to followers in Rome.

"Wish good for those who do bad things to you. Wish them well and do not curse them.

Be happy with those who are happy. Be sad with those who are sad.

Live together in peace with each other.

Do not be proud, but make friends with those who seem unimportant.

Do not think how clever you are.

If someone does wrong to you, do not pay him back by doing wrong to him.

Try to do what everyone thinks is right.

Do your best to live in peace with everyone." Romans 12:14-18 ICB

Be happy with those who
are happy. Be sad with
those who are sad.

Romans 12:15 ICB

NEW TESTAMENT

Chapter 17: From the Bible books of Romans, 1 Corinthians, 2 Corinthians, Galatians, Ephesians, Philippians, Colossians and Thessalonians

Paul's tough letters

INTRODUCTION

This chapter guides us through some of the letters Paul wrote to different groups of Christians.

The style in the letters seems sometimes quite sharp and stern. Paul wanted to bring people to their senses, or bring them back to the beliefs and ways of living that he had taught them. In these following pages we read of Paul calling the Christians at Corinth "babies", and telling them off for boasting.

Paul gives plenty of positive advice as well. Writing to the Christians at Galatia he lists the things that they should not do and then lists nine qualities they should have in their lives.

In his letter to the Ephesians Paul tells his readers the sorts of things they should not say, and then the sorts of things they should say.

Paul gives great words of encouragement in his first letter to the Thessalonians, as they face their troubles without him.

A right telling off

274

WHO IS PAUL?

Paul never met Jesus in person. In fact, Paul had once hated the Christians and everything they did. He spied on them, hunted them down, and even handed them over to the Romans to be put in prison or killed.

Then one day Paul had an amazing vision. He saw a blinding light, and in a flash, Paul heard Jesus speaking directly to him. Paul became a believer who was willing to risk his own life for Jesus. He travelled all over the Roman Empire sharing the good news about Jesus Christ.

Some of Jesus' followers had a lot to learn. The apostle Paul, who had been a top rabbi, was an excellent teacher.

And so, brothers and sisters, I could not speak to you as spiritual people, but . . . as infants in Christ.

1 Corinthians 3:1

1 Corinthians chapter 3 verses 1 to 9, and chapter 4 verses 8 to 17

"How you boast!"

CHRISTIANS AT CORINTH

Writing to new followers of Jesus in the town of Corinth, Paul had a lot of wrongs to put right.

"You're living like all the wicked people around you," Paul challenged them. "When I visited you," Paul continued, "I had to treat you like little babies. And even now, you are behaving like babies, not like the age you are.

"How you love to boast," Paul continued. "You act as if you were strong and rich but you are really feeble and poor when it comes to trusting God. While you go around saying how strong you are, we are weak."

"Look at us," said Paul. "People curse us, but we bless them. They hurt us, and we accept it."

We are hungry and thirsty, we are poorly clothed and beaten and homeless.

1 Corinthians 4:11

New ways to live

276

A LITTLE NEW YEAST

"Your boasting will get you nowhere," warned Paul.

"You know that just one spoonful of new yeast mixed into a big bowl of dough causes the dough to rise and become good loaves of bread."

"You've got to get rid of the old yeast in your lives. Then you will be like a new batch of dough.

"Remember," continued Paul, "Jesus is the one who died to make us good and to make us pure."

LOVE IS . . .

Even if I could speak like an angel, if I didn't have love I'd be like a clanging gong. I could be a genius, a superhero, or even a saint, but if I didn't have love, what good would that be?

Love is patient and kind. Love is not envious. It doesn't boast or insist on its own way. Love is not

It is written: "He scatters abroad; he gives to the poor; his righteousness endures for ever."

2 Corinthians 9:9

irritable or resentful. It doesn't laugh at bad news, but is happy when people are truthful. Love puts up with anything. Love believes. And love hopes.

Fine speeches come to an end, but love never ends.

BE GENEROUS

"You Corinthians must give generously," stated Paul, "especially since I've told our fellow-Christians in Macedonia about your generosity. And make sure that, whatever you give, you give with joy."

Then after three years I did go up to Jerusalem to meet with Cephas [Peter] and stayed with him fifteen days.

Galatians 1:18

Paul's tough letter

"LISTEN TO ME"

"You've got to listen to my teaching, you Christians of Galatia," insisted Paul. "It's not that I'm boasting, it's because God has given me a message that you must accept. You see, my sermons and letters are not full of my own thoughts and ideas. Rather, they are God's wisdom that has been given to me."

MY MESSAGE IS FROM GOD

"After my moment of hearing Jesus speak to me on the road to Damascus, I didn't rush off to Jerusalem and learn from the other disciples. No. I was taught directly by God. So what I now say comes from God."

For I want you to know, brothers and sisters, that the gospel that was proclaimed by me is not of human origin.

Galatians 1:11

PETER GETS IT WRONG

"Even Peter gave in to those who wanted new believers to obey the old Jewish laws," Paul continued. "As soon as Jews came on the scene Peter would no longer eat with non-Jewish people. I spoke to him face to face: 'Peter, why are you now saying that non-Jews must obey Jewish laws? You're wrong!' You must see it, you Galatians; the only thing that matters is our faith in Jesus."

280

Lists about how to live

Paul give three other lists in his letters about how Jesus' followers are meant to live.

2 Corinthians
In his second letter to the Christians at Corinth Paul says, "We show that we are servants of God by living a pure life, by our understanding, by our patience, and by our kindness . . . by true love, by speaking the truth . . ." (2 Corinthians 6:6, 7 ICB).

Ephesians
"Always be humble and gentle. Be patient and accept each other with love" (Ephesians 4:2 ICB).

Colossians
"Show mercy to others; be kind, humble, gentle, and patient. Do not be angry with each other, but forgive each other. If someone does wrong to you, then forgive him" (Colossians 3:12, 13 ICB).

Two ways

"Let me tell you about two ways of living, fellow-Christians who live in Galatia," wrote Paul.

THE WRONG WAY

"The wrong things the sinful self does are clear . . . not being pure . . . worshipping false gods, witchcraft, hating, making trouble, being jealous, being angry, being selfish, making people angry with each other, causing divisions among people, having envy, being drunk, having wild and wasteful parties . . . I warned you before: those who do these things will not be in God's kingdom." Galatians 5:19-21 ICB

Galatians chapter 5 verses 19 to 26

THE RIGHT WAY

"The right way to live, as a follower of Jesus," continued Paul, "is to live under the control of God and the Spirit. The Spirit gives love, joy, peace, patience, kindness, goodness, faithfulness, gentleness, self-control.

"Our new life comes from the Spirit, so we follow the Spirit and are guided by the Spirit."

If we live by the Spirit, let us also be guided by the Spirit.

Galations 5:25

281

Paul writes to the Ephesians

282

*Put away from you all
bitterness and wrath and
anger and wrangling.*

Ephesians 4:31

WHEN YOU TALK

"This is how you should speak," wrote Paul to the Ephesians. "Do not say harmful things. But say what people need — words that will help others become stronger."

"Do not be bitter or angry or cross. Never shout angrily or say things to hurt others.

FORGIVE

"Never do anything evil. Be kind and loving to each other.

"Forgive each other just as God forgave you in Christ."

TAKE CARE HOW YOU LIVE

"Be very careful how you live." (4:29, 31-32; 5:15 ICB)

Ephesians chapter 4 verses 29 to 32, and chapter 5 verses 15 to 20

"Do not live like those who are not wise. Live wisely.

"I mean that you should use every chance you have for doing good, because these are evil times . . .

"Do not be drunk with wine . . . But be filled with the Spirit."

SAYING THANKS TO GOD

"Speak to each other with psalms, hymns, and spiritual songs. Sing and make music in your hearts to the Lord. Always give thanks to God the Father for everything." (5:16-20 ICB)

Be filled with the Spirit, as you sing psalms and hymns and spiritual songs among yourselves.

Ephesians 5:18-19

284

Advice to the Christians at Philippi

KEEP GOING

"This is what you, my dear friends who live in Philippi, should do," wrote Paul.

"Keep on working out your salvation. Do this with fear and trembling, because you are in God's presence. And remember that God is with you and works in you to help you obey him. He gives you the desire and the ability to do what you should."

BE A STAR

"Do everything without grumbling or arguing," continued Paul.

"Look around you. You live in a wicked world with wicked people doing evil things. You must shine like stars in this world."

. . . so that you may be blameless and innocent, children of God.

Philippians 2:15

Philippians chapter 2 verses 12 to 16, and Colossians chapter 1 verses 10 to 14

Paul's letters

Paul wrote 13 letters. He wrote nine letters to groups of Christians who lived in one area or city: Galatians, 1 Thessalonians, 2 Thessalonians, 1 Corinthians, 2 Corinthians, Romans, Colossians, Ephesians and Philippians. There are four letters to individuals: Philemon, 1 Timothy, 2 Timothy and Titus. Five of these letters were written while under house arrest in Rome (Ephesians, Colossians, Philemon and Philippians); 2 Timothy was written from a dungeon.

285

. . . so that you may lead lives worthy of the Lord, fully pleasing to him, as you bear fruit in every good work and as you grow in the knowledge of God.

Colossians 1:10

Paul's letter to the Colossians

BE FRUITFUL

"My dear fellow-believers who live in Colossae, this is how you must live:

"You've got to live the kind of life that pleases Jesus and brings him honour.

"You've got to be like trees from which people pick lots and lots of fresh, juicy fruit. The kind of fruit I'm talking about is doing good and growing in your understanding of God."

GOD'S POWER

"You'll be able to do all this," said Paul, "only if you rely on God and God's great power. He will make you so strong inside that you will be able to do all this."

Paul's first letter to the Christians at Thessalonica

286

*Paul, Silvanus, and
Timothy. To the church
of the Thessalonians . . .
Grace to you and peace.*

1 Thessalonians 1:1

TROUBLES

Paul founded a church in the city of Thessalonica. All the members were new followers of Jesus. He had to leave them suddenly, so he dashed off this letter to help them.

PERSECUTION

Paul knew that these new Christians would face many troubles and difficulties, so he wrote to encourage them in their faith in Jesus.

"We sent Timothy to strengthen and comfort you in your faith. We sent him so that none of you would

Letter writing

Who is the letter from?
If we don't recognize the postmark, or the handwriting, or the address at the top of the letter, the first thing we do when we open a letter is to see who it is from. We have to go right to the end of the letter to find this out. But in Paul's day, you were told who the letter was from at the start of the letter. So Paul starts his letter, "From Paul, Silvanus, and Timothy" (1 Thessalonians 1:1).

Who is the letter to?
Next, the letter says who it is addressed to:
"To the church in Thessalonica . . ."

In Paul's day, letters gave a greeting. Paul wrote a Christian form of greeting to the Thessalonians: "Grace to you and peace."

be upset by these troubles we have now. You yourselves know that we must have these troubles. Even when we were with you, we told you that we would all have to suffer. And you know that it has happened the way we said. This is why I sent Timothy to you, so that I could know about your faith." (3:2-5 ICB)

Aspire to live quietly, to mind your own affairs, and to work with your hands, as we directed you.

1 Thessalonians 4:11

1 Thessalonians chapter 5 verses 1 to 11

Jesus will return

288

BE READY

Some Christians believed that Jesus would soon come back to be with them. When that didn't happen they got discouraged. But Paul assured them, "The day will come when we least expect it. The day will come as a thief does, in the middle of the night, when we are least expecting it.

BE ARMED

"So keep alert. Be prepared for Jesus' return," continued Paul.

"We're in a battle against evil. In battles, warriors wear clothes to protect themselves. In this battle, you need faith and love to protect you. And on your head you should put the helmet called "the hope of salvation".

For you yourselves know very well that the day of the Lord will come like a thief in the night.

1 Thessalonians 5:2

NEW TESTAMENT

Chapter 18: From the Bible books of 2 Thessalonians, 1 Timothy, 2 Timothy, Titus, Philemon and James

Paul's tender letters

INTRODUCTION

Some Christians at Thessalonica stopped working because they thought Jesus was about to return. A letter from Paul sets them straight — "Keep doing what is right."

In Paul's two letters to Timothy we see how fond the writer was of Timothy. And the young Timothy gets lots of advice on the importance of prayer, on what to look for in a good church leader, on the lure of money, and on the value of the Scriptures. Also included in this book are some of the last words written by Paul.

The letter to Titus contains more friendly advice from Paul, while a letter from Paul to Philemon makes a request for a loving welcome on behalf of a runaway slave.

This book ends with down-to-earth teaching from James — about caring for poor people and controlling your anger.

"Keep working"

Some of the Christians at Thessalonica had stopped working. "If Jesus is coming back so soon, why bother?" they thought. "We can all just go home and wait for the end of the world to happen."

They had the wrong idea, and Paul wrote a second letter to the church in Thessalonica to get this sorted out.

KEEP CLEAR

"People who refuse to work aren't following the teaching that we gave to you," Paul explains. "Sisters and brothers, you should keep away from other believers who are acting in this way."

PAUL'S EXAMPLE

Paul was a tentmaker. He was skilful at stitching together the heavy canvas. When Paul visited Christians in other

Now we command you, beloved, in the name of our Lord Jesus Christ, to keep away from believers who are living in idleness and not according to the tradition that they received from us.

2 Thessalonians 3:6

2 Thessalonians chapter 3 verses 7 to 13

cities, he took his work with him. This way, he earned money to help pay for his room and board.

"Don't forget the example that we gave you," the letter continues. "You should copy us. We were not lazy when we visited you. When we ate someone else's food, we always paid for it."

MY OWN HAND

The letter ends with the curious note: "See I am writing with my own hand." Paul usually dictated his letters to a friend who wrote them down for him. But at the end he would sometimes add a note in his own handwriting. This was to prove that the letter came from him, and not from someone pretending to be him.

We did not eat anyone's bread without paying for it; but with toil and labour we worked night and day, so that we might not burden any of you.

2 Thessalonians 3:8

Letters to Timothy

292

A GROWING CHURCH

On his final missionary journey, Paul went again to Ephesus. When Paul left, Timothy stayed behind to carry on Paul's work. One of Timothy's jobs was to find and train leaders for the young church in Ephesus. But Timothy was himself young and in need of help. Paul wrote two letters to encourage and teach him.

MY CHILD

"Timothy, you are like my own special child. Don't be timid. Be a good leader in the church. Do all the things that we know you can do. It is as though we're in a military battle. We're in a struggle about faith, and we have to keep a firm grip on what we believe."

I am giving you these instructions, Timothy my child . . . so that by following them you may fight the good fight.

1 Timothy 1:18

293

I want men everywhere
to pray. These men who
lift up their hands in
prayer must be holy.
They must not be men
who become angry and
have arguments.

1 Timothy 2:8 ICB

Timothy

Timothy may have become
a Christian as a result of
Paul's visit to Lystra (in
modern-day Turkey) where
he grew up. He joined Paul
for Paul's second, third and
fourth dangerous missionary
journeys, and was with Paul
during the two-year house
arrest in Rome. Paul wrote
to the Philippians,
"Timothy's worth you know,
how like a son with a father
he has served with me in
the work of the gospel"
(2:22). In six of his letters,
Paul sends greetings from
Timothy.

Throughout the
centuries, Christians who
have found the going tough
have been spurred on by
Paul's words to Timothy.

PRAYER

"Now, Timothy, I want to tell you about praying to
God:

Pray for everyone, because God doesn't leave
anyone out. God wants everyone to know the truth.

Don't hold up angry fists. Instead, hold your
hands up in prayer.

Don't dress up in fancy clothes when
you go to pray. It's far more
important to do things that
please God. Help other
people, especially the
poor."

More advice for the church

Let deacons . . . manage their children and their households well.

1 Timothy 3:12

WHAT MAKES A GOOD CHURCH LEADER? New Testament writers refer to two types of church leaders — overseers (also called elders or bishops) and deacons. Overseers preached, taught and guided the church; deacons (the word means "people who serve") helped in the practical, everyday care of Christians.

This letter describes what makes a good leader: "Good church leaders are gentle, wise, and calm. They aren't violent or aggressive."

1 Timothy chapter 3 verses 1 to 13, and chapter 6 verses 6 to 10

*For the love of money is a root of all kinds of evil,
and in their eagerness to be rich some have
wandered away from the faith.*

1 Timothy 6:10

"Church leaders must care well for their own families. If they can't do that, how can they possibly care for the church family?

"Good leaders are people that others trust and respect. They welcome other people into their homes. They're not conceited. They take what they do seriously. They don't lie or put other people down. They aren't greedy for money."

MONEY MATTERS

"Let's get it straight about money. If we have our basic needs, like enough food to eat and clothes to wear, we should be contented people.

"People who long to become rich fall into a trap. People who want to be rich are swamped by temptation. They run after lots of foolish things, which only gives them trouble. Wanting to have lots and lots of money has made some people stop following Jesus. In the end, having a great love for money only brings sadness."

Timid Timothy

296

TIMOTHY'S FAITH

Paul wrote his second letter to Timothy from a dungeon in Rome.

"Timothy, I miss you very much, just as you miss me. How I recall our tearful goodbye. I long to see you again. That would make me full of joy.

"I remember you all the time in my prayers, both night and day.

"I know that your faith is strong. This is the same faith that your mother, Eunice, and your grandmother

I am reminded of your sincere faith, a faith that lived first in your grandmother Lois and your mother Eunice and now, I am sure, lives in you.

2 Timothy 1:5

Lois, had. Timothy, remember to use the gift that God gave you when I laid my hands on your head. This special gift from God must grow. It must be like a tiny flame that is fanned into a fire.

"Don't be a timid Timothy. The spirit God has given us makes us brave. God's Spirit fills us with power and love and self-control."

A WORKER FOR GOD

"Now, Timothy, I know that you long to work for God. As God's worker, don't be embarrassed, and don't be ashamed because I'm a prisoner.

"A house is full of special things made of gold and silver. But it also has many things made of wood and clay. Think of yourself as one of those special things, to be used for something important."

In a large house there are utensils . . . some for special use, some for ordinary.

2 Timothy 2:20

The Scriptures

298

WISDOM

The second letter to
Timothy gave good
advice:

"Continue to follow what you have
learned, and remember what you have been
taught. You know that you can trust your
teachers."

Ever since he had been a child, Timothy had heard
the Hebrew Scriptures — the words of the prophets, the
psalms, the stories of Noah, Abraham, Sarah, Hagar, Joseph,
Moses, Miriam, and all the others. This is what Paul says about
the sacred Jewish writings:

"All these sacred texts, given by God, teach us how to live. God has
breathed wisdom into the words. They make us wise enough to put our
trust in Jesus, who makes us whole."

From childhood you have known the sacred
writings that are able to instruct you.

2 Timothy 3:15

2 Timothy chapter 3 verses 14 to 17, and chapter 4 verses 9 to 18

Final words

Paul has some final, personal words: "Apart from Luke, I am all alone here in prison. When I first went on trial, no one helped me. In fact, everyone deserted me. But the Lord was with me and gave me strength.

"I beg you, come and see me just as soon as you can. And when you come, bring my friend Mark along with you. He's a very useful person to have around. It's freezing here in prison, so please bring my coat with you, the one I left with Carpus.

"And when you come, bring those scrolls of mine — the ones which have scriptures written on them.

"I'm about to leave this world, my dear friend. May the Lord bring me safely to his kingdom in heaven. Goodbye and may the Lord be with you."

When you come, bring the cloak I left with Carpus at Troas, also the books, and above all the parchments.

2 Timothy 4:13

A letter to Titus

300

WHO IS TITUS?

Titus was another of Paul's friends and helpers. Titus often travelled with Paul as he went from city to city telling people about Jesus. Titus delivered one of Paul's letter to Christians in the city of Corinth.

Paul had given Titus the task of teaching the Christians on Crete. Later, he wrote this letter to Titus setting out guidelines and priorities.

ADVICE

"Titus, you are like a true son to me. Here is some advice to help you and others in the church:

"Choose overseers to be in charge of God's work. They should be good role models, doing what is right. They should be strong in faith, in love, and in patience.

"Remember that God loves us just because he is kind, not because of what we do. We don't earn God's love: it's a free gift."

Teach older women . . .
not to speak against
others.

Titus 2:3 ICB

Philemon

Paul wrote this letter to a man named Philemon. The person who delivered the letter for Paul was a runaway slave named Onesimus.

My dear friend Philemon,

Whenever I pray for you, I always thank God. I keep hearing how loving you are. It's love like yours that keeps me going here in prison. Because I love you, I am asking you for a favour.

Onesimus ran away from you. He has been helping me in prison. He has become

like a son to me, and I wish he could stay. I am sending him back to you, and now I am asking that he may no longer be your slave, but your brother.

So welcome him as you would welcome me. And while I think of it, can you get your guest room ready for me too. As soon as I get out of prison, I want to visit you.

Love, Paul

Teaching from James

302

LOOKING INTO A MIRROR

People who hear God's word but don't do anything are like those who look at themselves in a mirror and instantly forget what they look like. They may have

For if any are hearers of the word and not doers, they are like those who look at themselves in a mirror . . .

James 1:23

messy hair or jam on their nose. But they look away and do nothing about it. What good is that? It's the same with faith. Faith without loving action is useless. You must be doers of the word, not just hearers.

For if a person with gold
rings and in fine clothes
comes into your assembly,
and if a poor person in dirty
clothes also comes in . . .

James 2:2

RICH PERSON, POOR PERSON

"You must never think that one person is more
important than another person," James continued in
his letter.

"Suppose two very different people arrive in your
meeting. The first one is dressed smartly in designer
clothes, with gold rings, gold bracelets and a silver watch. At the same time another
person arrives, with no jewellery, no watch. In place of fine clothes, the poor person
wears a threadbare overcoat, over torn jeans, and shoes full of holes.

"You rush up to the first one and say: 'Good morning, we're so pleased to see you.
Would you like to sit here in the best seat in the church?' But you practically ignore
the one in shabby clothes. 'I suppose you can come in. Just stand over there in the
corner where nobody will notice you.' Do not act like that."

James chapter 3 verses 1 to 12

Watch your tongue

304

"Your tongue may be one of the smallest parts of your body, but it is one of the most powerful," warned James in his letter.

"If you can control your tongue, you've managed to bring all of yourself under control. It's like a sailing ship set at full sail in a strong wind. Just the slightest push on the rudder and the whole boat changes course, even though the rudder is so tiny.

"Or think of a fire. From one little match a whole forest can be set ablaze. It's just like that with the tongue. It has the power to change a person's life, for better or worse. So tame your tongue. Use it to help people and to praise God."

How great a forest is set ablaze by a small fire! And the tongue is a fire.

James 3:5-6

Secrets from the book of Revelation

INTRODUCTION

This chapter dips into some of the shortest of the letters in the New Testament as well as into its most mysterious book, the book of Revelation.

Peter offers mature wisdom about how to serve God.

John speaks about light and love.

When he wrote Revelation, John was a prisoner on the island of Patmos because of his faith. He wrote words of encouragement, comfort and hope to Christians who were also facing persecution. But he wrote in a kind of code. He wrote to seven churches in Asia, encouraging them and also challenging them. And he shared a vision of hope, a time when troubles would end.

Adding to your faith

Peter

Peter was a fisherman when Jesus called him to be a disciple and he quickly became the leader of the Twelve. Later, Jesus said to Peter, "Feed my sheep" — that is, "Take care of my followers." And that is the purpose of these two letters. Peter writes to encourage Christians and to help them deal with attacks on their faith. Unlike his second letter, Peter's first letter is written in stylish Greek — not the sort of Greek you'd expect from a Galilean fisherman. This puzzle is solved by Peter's words in 1 Peter 5:12: he wrote "with the help of Silas".

"What are the things that, when added to each other, equal a strong follower of Jesus?" asked Peter at the start of his second letter.

"I'll tell you: You start with having faith in Jesus.

To this faith, add goodness.

To your goodness, add knowledge.

To your knowledge, add self-control.

To your self-control, add the ability to keep going.

To your ability to keep going, add devotion to God.

To your devotion to God, add kindness to other followers of Jesus.

To your kindness to other followers of Jesus, add love.

"Once all these things are part of you, you will know more about Jesus, and you will be a good worker for him. And don't forget this. It was God who chose you to be followers in the first place. So keep working hard to make it clear that God has called you."

"If you remember these things you won't fail. If you act on them you will be part of the kingdom that Jesus promises. I'll do my best to keep reminding you. You must never forget these things."

For this very reason, you must make every effort to support your faith with goodness.

2 Peter 1:5

Walking in the light

GOD IS LIGHT

"This is the message we had from God. Now we are passing it on to you," wrote John at the start of his first letter. "God is light. There is no hint of darkness about God.

"This means that if we say we are God's friends yet often do bad things, then we are plain stupid, and lying through our teeth. While we pretend to be walking in the light, we are really stumbling along in the dark."

This is the message we have heard from him and proclaim to you, that God is light.

1 John 1:5

1 John chapter 1 verses 5 to 10, and chapter 2 verses 7 to 11

Whoever loves a brother
or sister lives in the
light, and in such a
person there is no cause
for stumbling.

1 John 2:10

HOW TO LIVE IN THE LIGHT

"Someone might say, 'I live in the light, I'm a really good person.' But let me tell you — if you hate others, you are walking in the dead of night. If you hate friends, other followers of Jesus, or everyone in sight, you don't have any idea what it's like to walk in the light. You're lost in total darkness. You trip and stumble and hurt yourself because you can't see where you are going. You're like a child, wearing a blindfold and bumping into all the furniture."

Good and evil

LOVE EACH OTHER

"I'm not writing anything new to you. You've had this teaching from the time you first followed Jesus. In a nutshell, we must love each other," continued John in his first letter.

CAIN AND ABEL

"Do you remember that story in the Hebrew Scriptures about Cain and Abel? Cain did many evil things. Cain hated his brother so much that he killed him. Why did he do this? Because Abel did good things. You must in no way be like Cain, who lived in the grip of the Evil One."

God is love, and those who abide in love abide in God, and God abides in them.

1 John 4:16

311

YOU WILL BE HATED

"So don't be surprised when you meet people in the world today like Cain. You may very well find yourself hated just because you do good. But we know that we have left the realm of death and have crossed over the bridge into the realm of life. We know this because of our love for other followers of Jesus.

"If you don't love, then you still live in the land of darkness. And if you hate your brother or sister, then you are no better than Cain. But we show that we are loving people by the good that we do."

HOW TO BE A CONQUEROR

In the last chapter of John's first letter, chapter 5, verse 5, he writes: "Who is it that conquers the world but the one who believes that Jesus is the Son of God?" (NRSV)

I write to you, young people, because you are strong and the word of God abides in you.

1 John 2:14

The church in Ephesus

The book of Revelation

A time of persecution
Revelation, the last book in the Bible, is mysterious and hard to understand. It was written in a time of terrible persecution. Christians were being put in prison or killed. John was a prisoner himself when he wrote Revelation. He wanted to give hope and comfort, so people wouldn't give up.

John used many strange symbols, objects, and pictures. Sometimes he used a code. If people who hated Christians read it, they wouldn't understand it. We need to de-code it when we read it today.

The code
The name of the book "Revelation" means to uncover something. It discloses things about God.

Numbers
Numbers are symbolic. The number 7, for example, stands for perfection or completion. In this book you will find seven churches, seven angels, seven golden lampstands, seven trumpets, and seven crowns, among many other sevens.

Names of Jesus
This book has many different names for Jesus.

He is called: the faithful witness (1:5); the ruler of the kings of the earth (1:5); the Alpha [first] and the Omega [last] (1:8); the Lion (5:5); the Lamb (5:6); Lord of lords (17:14); King of kings (17:14).

SEVEN CHURCHES
This is the message of Jesus Christ to the seven churches in Asia: Ephesus, Smyrna, Pergamum, Thyatira, Sardis, Philadelphia, and Laodicea. "The first message is for the church of Ephesus:

"The One speaking to you [that is, the Lord Jesus Christ] walks among the seven golden lampstands [that is, the churches of Asia]. In my right hand of power and authority I hold seven stars [these are the angels of the seven churches]."

313

YOUR GOOD POINTS

"I've seen all the good things you do. I know how hard you work and that you never give up. I know that you have no time for evil people. You have uncovered those people who pretend to be apostles."

"Let anyone who has an ear listen to what the Spirit is saying to the churches."

Revelation 2:7

YOUR BAD POINTS

"But I do have some things against you. You don't love as strongly as you did at the beginning. So love as strongly as you used to. Start showing that love to other people. Anyone who has an car, listen to what the Spirit is saying."

The church in Smyrna

THE FIRST AND THE LAST

"This is the message to you who belong to the church in Smyrna: The One who is giving you this message is called the First and the Last. The One who is speaking to you is the One who was dead but is now alive again."

Revelation chapter 2 verses 8 to 11

*"These are the words of
the first and the last,
who was dead and
came to life."*

Revelation 2:8

Suffering

"I have nothing but good things to say to you about your strong faith in God. You're doing very well indeed. I know all about your troubles. You don't have a lot of money, but in faith terms you're millionaires. I know about those who are against you and about those untrue things they accuse you of. You will suffer, and some of you will be thrown into prison just because you are faithful followers of Jesus."

Martyrs

"Your suffering won't go on for ever. You may be imprisoned, but even if you are killed, you are to remain faithful to God. God will reward you in heaven with the crown of life."

The church in Pergamum

"This is the message to the church in Pergamum: The One who is speaking to you has a long two-edged sword, the sword of judgement."

"Write this to the angel of the church in Pergamum: The One who has the sharp two-edged sword says this to you."

Revelation 2:12 ICB

WELL DONE

"I know all about the tough place where you live, which is like living in Satan's city where Satan sits on the throne. But you have not given in and have remained true to me. Even when one Christian became a martyr, you still spoke out bravely about your faith in me. Very well done."

Revelation chapter 2 verses 12 to 17

YOU COULD DO BETTER

"But I do have a few things against you. There are some of you who follow evil teaching. This false teaching is like the teaching of Balaam, who led people away from God. You've got to put a stop to following this kind of teaching."

YOUR REWARD

"Each one of you who stays faithful to me will have a great reward. In heaven you will feed on special food, like the manna God's people ate in the desert. You will also be given a white stone. On the white stone is written a secret name. This stone will be your ticket into heaven. Only you will know what name is on the stone. It will be your own new name."

The church in Laodicea

"This is the message to the seventh church in Asia, the church in Laodicea: The One giving you this message is called 'Amen'. He is a faithful and true witness. He rules over everything that God has made."

LUKEWARM

"I have to tell you off for some of your serious faults. You are just like the pathetic water supply in the town of Laodicea which dries up so often. You are not hot or cold. Your love for me is wishy-washy; it's not one thing or the other. I'm going to spit you out of my mouth like disgusting, lukewarm water.

"You swagger around town boasting about how rich you are. Because you have money you think that's all you need. But when it comes to serving God and loving him, you are at the bottom of the league. You are like a poor blind person who has to beg for food and clothes."

BUY GOLD

"This must be your plan of action: buy gold from me. This gold will have been purified by fire. Then you will be rich in the spirit. Buy white clothes. Then you will be forgiven. Buy special medicine to cure your blindness, then you will see things as God sees them." Of course, the writer didn't mean that Christians should literally go shopping. Rather they needed to say they were sorry and to start living in God's way.

KNOCKING ON THE DOOR

"And, remember, I'm only correcting you because I love you so much. Change your lives. Change your hearts. I'm standing outside the door of your life. I'm knocking on the door. As you hear my voice, open up to me. Then I promise to come in, and I will sit down and have a good meal with you."

"I know your works; you are neither cold nor hot."

Revelation 3:15

Revelation chapter 21 verses 1 to 6, and chapter 22 verses 1 to 5

New heaven and earth

320

The writer of Revelation wrote of a time when troubles and persecution would end. Everything would be different.

"I see a new heaven and a new earth. The old heaven and earth have gone, and so has the sea of trouble. God is living right beside us. He will wipe away our tears. There will be no more pain or crying.

"A river, clear as crystal, will flow through our city. The tree of life will grow on its banks, bearing fruit not just once a year but every month, so no one will ever be hungry. What's more, this tree has leaves that heal every hurt.

"The throne of God and the Lamb (Jesus) will be there. God's servants will see him face to face. God's name will be written on their foreheads."

On either side of the river is the tree of life.

Revelation 22:2